Hidden World

The Inside Story of the Soul

Published by Brolga Publishing Pty Ltd
ABN 46 063 962 443
PO Box 12544
A'Beckett St
Melbourne,VIC, 8006
Australia

email: markzocchi@brolgapublishing.com.au

National Library of Australia
Cataloguing-in-Publication data

Kaushik Ram, author.
Title: Hidden World : The Inside Story of the Soul
ISBN: 9781925367867 (paperback)
Subjects: Paradox.
Fallacies (Logic).
Thought and thinking.
Truth.
Self.
Intentionality (Philosophy)

Cover design by - Alice Cannet
Typesetting by - Elly Cridland

Hidden World

The Inside Story of the Soul

Dr. Kaushik Ram

Contents

Dedication

Preface

PART ONE - Healing of Humanity

Freedom of Forgiveness ... 1

Strength of Vulnerability ... 17

Embodiment of Truth ... 25

PART TWO – Intelligence of the Unknown

Honouring the Body ... 41

Intelligence of the Moment ... 67

Flow State ... 85

PART THREE – Fathomless Magic

The 7 Principles of Magic ... 109

Prayer of the Heart ... 111

The Rewards of Risk ... 131

Gift of Service ... 143

Journey of Remembering ... 159

Epilogue ... 183

Dedication

This book is wholeheartedly dedicated to the hands that first held me; the hands that raised me; the hands that I'm yet to hold in my own and forever honour that without them, I wouldn't be who I am. Through my parents' love I shine.

Preface

Once a golden bird was captured by a forest nymph. In truth, it was the nymph who was captured by the beauty of the golden bird. Spellbound, the nymph forgot the love of all things and became envious of the love that the other forest creatures had for the golden bird. And so the golden bird was kept in a cage at the nymph's dwelling. Deprived of its freedom the golden bird died. The nymph was consumed by terrible loss. Then the nymph saw she was simply kindling her heart's flame with snow. Without a cure for the troubles of her heart, she decided to rid this world of love, so no-one else would commit the crime she had. She cast a spell that forbade love from men's hearts.

Without the warmth of love, the hearts of men became restless. The magic of love was thought of as if it were a ghost, a ghost that everyone talked about but no one had ever seen. It was then that the nymph understood that if the bees were not attracted to the flower, there would be no honey. The bees do not collect flowers, they simply collect the nectar. The nymph saw that love isn't unforgiving, it wasn't a crime in the first place. Still, love was a magic too powerful. The nymph decided that her curse would be lifted only when men understood surrender. The nymph decided that it would be at sunrise and sunset that we would learn of surrender. And so men contemplated the sunrise without ever thinking of possessing it, neither did we stop the sun from setting.

So it was, that men named love, to live by the sun and love by the moon. But love was never meant to be defined. This is perhaps why love prefers twilight.

Part One

Healing of Humanity

Our chronically thinking minds have become a magnet for reason in a sea of doubt. It is futile to find purpose when the evolution of humankind has been hijacked by fear. Is the human soul more than just an evolutionary experiment in survival? We begin by exposing that which occludes the unseen.

The Freedom Of Forgiveness

Rest in natural great peace
this exhausted mind
beaten helplessly by karma
and neurotic thoughts
like the relentless fury of
the pounding waves
in the infinite ocean of Samsara
Rest in natural great peace
to find rest
to rest
Rest

~ Nyoshul Khenpo Rinpoche

How can our children be free of the human condition when their fire burns with the flame of pain, fear, rejection and shame? Although we inherit the suffering of generations before us, we are to learn the lessons of our grandfathers and grandmothers for ourselves. Those lessons are never new and since the suffering continues its cycle with each generation, we begin by forgiving. Our forefathers are not to blame for a world that is unjust. It is through forgiveness that we free ourselves from the human condition. It is then that we see that we have been misled by an illusion; an illusion that exists as long as we expect the world to be as we think.

Illusions are not only found inside the mind but exist viscerally as entities in our bodies. Illusions are to the mind what entities are to the body. These entities exist as the heaviness that sits on our chest when we carry anger; the tragedy and guilt that keep the stomach churning. These entities may exist within us without our knowledge. For some, these entities become identities of the subconscious. We may never know what is in our subconscious, yet it is the subconscious that reveals itself in the patterns we see in our lives. The subconscious that has already decided our thoughts before we think.

Take the young artist who cannot understand why she regards herself with such low esteem. Whenever she gets offered an exhibition for her work, she kindly declines saying that she will think about it. In fact, she thinks about it for days on end. She talks herself down. Who is she to pretend that she is refined in her art? She comes from an abusive family. She didn't know her father and her mother treated her as if she was to blame for the atrocities she finds in her life. The young woman escapes to distant lands to leave her past behind. Her journey is quick to show her that pain only attracts more suffering. She learns that life teaches her lessons: sacred lessons, lessons of pleasure, lessons of pain, lessons that happen for a reason and those that happen without. Until one day she realises that lessons are things that she has created explanations for. Sometimes we call the unavoidable a tragedy. At the end of her journey, she decides to heal the relationship with her mother. She asks her mother the questions that tormented her childhood. Did her mother vent her lack of control on her because she couldn't be alone with herself? Was it because her mother felt helpless when mistreated by her own parents? Her mother refuses to talk about the past which has no meaning.

The day comes when her mother is weakened by age and relocated to a nursing home. While packing the boxes, the young woman comes across letters written long ago. The letters talk about a little girl who had the face of her grandfather, a man who had betrayed their family and left her mother without a father. Her mother could not withhold hate and resentment each time she looked into her daughter's eyes. The young artist heals the pain passed on to her. The pain trapped in her subconscious that replicated the patterns of a lost father, with each generation. It is this pain that leads her in search of the love she never knew in her own home; the journey on which she goes is supported by those who healed wounds of their own. The young woman has nothing but love for her great mother, for no parent has ever failed their child. By forgiving the past, we learn to heal our wounds. This healing breaks the illusions of low self-worth. Gone are the entities that spoke of self-loathing each time she was shown love. Gone are the entities that told her that she was not good enough to live life in all its splendour. The young woman frees herself from the burden of inherited identity. She ends the cycle of resentment she had inherited from a past that was not hers to choose. She now understands why she so desperately tried to escape the conditions she was raised in. She realises that by lowering herself, not only did she disrespect herself but also she disrespected others by not sharing the best of herself. Her mother knows nothing of the healing that has taken place in her daughter. For reasons not yet apparent to her, the artist's mother feels freed from the psychological chords that trigger the rejection of men. By forgiving once, we have forgiven all.

No individual is immune to absorbing entities from the collective. As long as we belong to a collective identity, we will be the minority. Yet, we cannot deny the purity of our consciousness. The purity that emerges on rare moments when the weight of despair becomes suddenly profound. Disease, dense emotions and corrosive thoughts are psychological entities that have become visceral. They are so deeply embedded in the subconscious that it is not our voice but the voice of the entity that speaks through us. The entity separates itself from others by creating an identity. This identity speaks of what they think, who they are and what they want to be. It cannot be argued with. It defends the entities it is possessed by and avoids that which conflicts with itself. Yet, there will always be conflict. It is separation that creates hostility.

Take the one who has played safe. His is the identity that fears change. He has got a typical job that gives security. He neither enjoys nor questions what he does. He has saved for retirement and is now numb to existence. He has lost interest in partnerships and claims to be happy spending the night alone; a hassle-free life waiting for an assured death. When we lose the strength to defend our identity, we often seek isolation.

For some, a moment of clarity breaks the illusion of identity. However, this is only temporary and soon the identity speaks again. The identity now lives in internal conflict. The identity fears the consequence of abandoning the human condition. The once-remembered purity is now hidden in the closet; its light a secret never to be exposed. The mask of identity is put back on.

Then there are those who can no longer hide, and choose to take a path of discovery, self-growth and healing. This too becomes an identity. This one speaks of healing the body and the mind, of the path back to love.

The identity speaks of balancing spirituality and silliness, professionalism and play, spontaneity and structure, discipline and freedom, projection and presence, learning and unlearning. The identity walks the fine line, neither being carried away by the spiritual dogma nor the practicalities of the physical dimension. Yet, there is nothing to learn, nothing to fix and nothing to heal. To surrender to the eternal would mean the end of duality; the end of identity. So they hide behind a well-balanced life because they do not know how to face the uncomfortable unknown.

For as long as identity exists, we forgive. We forgive for we did not have a choice in the matter. We forgive the identity that decided to be someone because they were told that they were not good enough. We forgive the identity that did not allow the collective trauma of childhood to become a story. We forgive the identity that was broken by misfortune and lost the hope of creating a new reality. We forgive the identity that is convinced that money, power and greed are the way forward for we were not there for them in their times of tragedy, or when they felt alone. We forgive those who live in the anxiety of being responsible for other people's problems; for we rely on others to take responsibility so we can rest knowing that everything is taken care of. We forgive those who have been consumed by self-pity, the ones who are convinced that no one understands their problems, yet are too terrified to speak up. We forgive the ones who will not allow the river of tears to flow, for their identity has made a decision to appear strong yet without vulnerability no one can ask for help. We forgive the ones who have hurt us because it is by forgiving them that we set ourselves free. We forgive because to carry the weight of judgment will only perpetuate the human condition. We forgive, for the very identity that promises to protect us is what prevents us from being free.

Forgive them for they know not what they do[1]. Most of all, we forgive ourselves, for it is when we forgive for no reason that we have truly forgiven.

1 From Biblical literature

Forbidden Love - Story of identity shock

He did what he had to. He had worked hard to be where he was. Having crumbled many times to the struggles of life, he had built a fail-proof safety net that allowed him to explore emotions at a safe distance. He was successful in the eyes of others, celebrating life in all its abundance. He faced his challenges alone, outside the reach of others because he did not trust anyone to catch him when he fell. Yet his complication-free life was being questioned. A woman sat in front of him. Sarah had known Evan for three years. They had met at a launch party for a documentary film about rainforest conservation. It was July the 16th and it would be Evan's 32nd birthday tomorrow. Sarah had stopped over after work at his apartment in Sydney, Australia. She had bought him a box of artisan chocolate with his name engraved on each chocolate bar. They sat on his bed drinking caffeine-free chai and Sarah asked him three questions:

'What are you grateful for?'

Evan was at the height of his career, he was financially secure. He had a big heart and devoted his time to his mental, physical and social health.

'I am grateful for my health' he said eventually. 'To be free in my body as I am in my mind. I am grateful to have wonderful friends like you who have my back and are my refuge in this bustling city.'

Sarah looked at him fondly. 'How can we better support you?'

This question softened Evan's heart. He let his guard down a little. He looked into Sarah's kind eyes. He had always had trouble receiving love. Even more so, he had enormous trouble asking for help. He would rather suffer on his own than ever ask for support. This was a part of himself that he had meticulously concealed from those around him. He kept his emotions at bay, never diving too deep so he could always remain unattached. His self-control was his safety net. A net that worked both ways: protecting him from hurt and shielding him from receiving love.

'I would like to be held without reason,' he said. 'I am too afraid to seek shelter in the arms of another. I feel that I am the one who always has to provide. It makes me less of a man if I am unable to do so.' With this, Evan lowered his eyes. He did not want to be brave and do it all alone anymore. 'I would like to learn how to ask,' he added quietly.

'Who would you like to forgive?' His heart had been broken open by the previous question. His hands began to tremble from memories that he had blocked out for the purposes of living in the present moment. Memories that were resurfacing as a tsunami of tears. Sarah patiently sat in her own harmony, without anticipation. Evan collapsed into her arms, sobbing uncontrollably. Sarah stroked his back soothingly and gently pulled herself away from him. Lifting his chin up with her tender hand, she looked deep into his hollow eyes. 'Tell me' she said intently. Evan reached deep into his memories to collect lost fragments of information…

It was January 2007 when Evan had pursued his interest in animal behaviour to a remote marine research laboratory in Northland, New Zealand. He was excited to work with a professor who he looked up to. His research involved non-human senses such as electroreception and infrared vision. The research lab was located at the edge of a cliff, surrounded by ocean and the pristine New Zealand countryside. The nearby town had a rough population of 150, made up of mostly staff and students from the lab. The students of the lab occupied various roles in the town such as running the fire station and local radio. Evan lived on site at the lab, so he took up the responsibility of lab security, making sure everything was locked and turned off each night. The small number of people at the lab meant that they all got to know each other. There was strong unity amongst the students with regular BBQs on the beach and social drinks at the only pub in town.

This was the first time Evan had been on his own. He managed to survive the education system where he was told what to think, what to do and what to become, because we know what is best for our children. Evan studied to become what the education system promised. When he came out the other side, he realised there was no golden job waiting for him. In fact no one cared how much he had studied and yet again he was to prove himself like countless others who were doing the same. Like donkeys who do not question whether they are carrying firewood or gold, he had never questioned what it meant to climb the ladder of success. The ladder that gives the illusion of reaching the top, only to find that the ladder of success has no end. Instead, we are to keep climbing because everyone else is climbing and we don't want to fall behind. To this Evan had little concern because he was yet to think for himself. He did as he was told because his achievements had taught him that hard work paid off.

When Evan arrived at the research lab, he carried with him the questions that he was yet to discover. On the surface, he was of a quiet nature, obsessively observant and overly friendly. However, when things didn't go his way, he would act out the residual emotional patterns that were set aside in the relentless drive to the top. The false hierarchy he had acquired from a culture that gave prestige to the educated meant that he had a distorted relationship with people. It was his work that saved him from social awkwardness. He worked mostly in isolation doing brain surgery on small Carpet sharks to manipulate their behaviour.

One of the students at the lab was on a six-month overseas exchange programme from Russia. Evan got along well with Anna since they were both new to the research lab. She was light-hearted, funny, and outrageously honest. Sometimes she looked embarrassed immediately after she spoke her mind. Evan secretly admired these qualities in her. They hung out on social occasions yet didn't spend any time together by themselves. She had spoken of her German boyfriend and Evan respected their relationship. However, as the months passed, Evan's admiration turned into infatuation. He had not been close to any girl before, let alone been in love. Even worse, he felt guilty to be in love. 'She has a boyfriend' is what he reminded himself. His education had not taught him what it meant to be a Man. He was a boy lost in a generation convinced by the false hopes of reaching the top of a success ladder. She was a free spirit, discovering the world. Evan didn't even consider himself equal as a human being or worthy of her affection. With a hairdo as awkward as his personality, Evan couldn't be more undesirable. The forbidden love, a tension between them. Evan started to distance himself from her. In his fast-track road to success, he had learnt nothing of dealing with the emotions growing inside of him.

It did not matter how much Evan hid his feelings, they did not go away. Instead, he could not stop thinking about Anna. Each moment, each conversation, each time he saw her face, he would memorise everything that happened between them and replay it over and over in his mind. Memories gave some meaning to his life, something to live for. It was as if Evan's entire life was a dream up to this point and love had woken him up. Very quickly the six months came to an end. Anna had her farewell party at the local pub but Evan made no attempt to be there. He couldn't say goodbye. Instead he kept busy with his work, alone, by himself. This was the way to deal with his problems. The next day, Evan found a note at his doorstep saying 'sorry I didn't see you last night - goodbye good friend'. Anna was gone and Evan felt a terrible loss. He went back to all the places in his memory where they hung out. But these memories became haunting episodes. Instead of looking forward to seeing Anna each day, Evan started to regret each day lost without her. In his desperation, he decided to tell Anna his secret: he was madly in love with her. That evening he distractedly locked up the lab and then, wrote her an email.

Evan wrote that if he died tomorrow, at least he would die knowing that he had told her how much he loved her. Evan told her how guilty he felt that he was in love. He told her that he hadn't been able to think properly for weeks. He told her that each moment seemed to slip by without him being there. 'All I can think about is you.' Evan told her all the things that he admired in her. He told her that he could not get her out of his mind.

Anna replied a few days later. She told him this was a big surprise and she didn't know what to say. She wrote that she was sorry, she didn't have the same feelings for him. But they could stay in touch as friends. Evan respected her decision, but his heart had other ideas. For the first time, his stainless heart began to crack like glass. Unable to hide his feelings, he decided that the only remedy for a broken heart was to love more. To love her whether she liked it or not.

As time went on, their email exchange became more frequent. The more Evan got to know Anna, the more he fell in love. He fell more and more in love with a woman he would never see again. With each email, Evan incurred the fear of losing her, of not hearing back from Anna. His love for her was a secret. No one could help him because no one would ever find out. Evan would cry each night for the next six months because of unrequited love. The more he missed her, the deeper the void grew in his heart. His heart became a bottomless pit. A well so deep that light could no longer reach the bottom. Evan was losing himself. He didn't know who he was anymore. Sometimes, all he wanted was his life to return to the way it was, before he had met Anna.

The worst year of Evan's life was drawing to an end. During the Christmas break Anna went to Ibiza. When Evan saw photos of her on social media partying on the beach, he became engulfed by jealousy and anger. Evan couldn't understand how Anna could go to Ibiza and not mention anything about this in her last email. Poisoned by love, Evan wrote an email to her with the hidden emotions that turned on him. He reacted in the way that had been conditioned by a culture based on hierarchy, imposing his superiority over her. Talking to her as if she had not lived to the standards that society leads us to believe. Evan demanded love as if it was his right, yet because he knew nothing of love, he also did not know what he was asking for.

Anna replied a few days later. She said that he had all the wrong ideas. She said she wasn't mad at him because she knew so damned well how it felt to be hurt. Reading her email, Evan began to drown in humiliation. His shame reached a point where his emotional pain became physical. Evan had never hurt himself in any way. But this was different. Evan's body was hurting him. It was as if his body had decided to self-destruct, to kill itself. Evan's body was rejecting life. Every cell in his body began to shut down. His face distorted like the shattered pieces of his heart. A gust of air filled the space that separated his body and his mind. Evan experienced all of this in horror, terrified of departing this world.

When he regained the slightest bit of control over his body, he ran out of the lab into the countryside, through the forest till he reached the edge of a ten-meter cliff. Jagged rocks lay below with the waves of the ocean pounding furiously. He started to descend down the cliff with little regard for his own life. He was hoping to slip and fall. Death would relieve him of his misery. To his dismay, he reached the bottom without harm. There he remained all night, beaten helplessly by karma, by the relentless fury of the pounding waves. It was approaching morning when he felt he had punished himself enough to convince himself to climb back up. The staff from the marine lab would start arriving and he had to pull himself together before anyone noticed his absence. Evan arrived back at the lab and frantically took a shower. Then he wrote to Anna.

He told her that he was not going to ask for forgiveness because he did not deserve to be forgiven. Evan told Anna that she meant more to him than his own life. He told her that he would work really hard to heal all this regret. He told her that he would try to move on with his life and repair himself as quickly as possible. There was no point feeling hurt or sorry for himself. The horrific taste of death had alerted him to the value of life. He must not waste a moment of the miracle that he has been gifted. This is what he thought.

In January 2008, Evan's contract with the marine lab ended. He returned to his parents' house. Without a job to distract him, guilt and self-pity began to surface from the depths of the well that had no light.

The false realities he had been deluding himself with became an entity that consumed his energy, feeding off his low self-worth. Evan could no longer hide behind the illusion of loving someone to escape from his own pain. The enormity of his pain compounded, haunting him with dreams that would never be fulfillled. The sleepless nights soaked his pillow with tears that knew no end. Each morning he would put his pillow in the sun to dry. Evan was trapped in desperation. He would do anything to see her once more. Each moment that he thought was a miracle, became the most hostile time to be alive. He had to escape at once. He decided that Australia would be the easiest place to escape to. As soon as he had enough confidence in his vague plans, Evan booked a flight. He had made up his mind. His life was tearing him apart and he could not let anyone know why. No one would understand him.

Evan arrived in Australia, carrying with him the baggage of his past. In a desperate cry for help in a land where he thought being alone would allow him to escape his loneliness, Evan wrote a letter asking for advice. He recollected his story and ended the letter with:

'Please tell me what to do with my life. Because no matter where I go or what I do, I remain restless and feel that my life is absolutely useless.'

Without a person in the world to send this letter to, Evan sent this letter to Anna out of habit. This time he did not get a reply from Anna. The reply instead came from someone named Izabella. It was a short reply:

'My name is Izabella and Anna asked me to write you something. I think it is best that the contact between you and her ends. You have to accept that she hasn't any feelings for you and concentrate on your own life. I really wish you the best for your life, but I think you have to forget Anna to be open for a new way in your life.'

Evan wasn't mad. He didn't even feel hurt when he read this. He simply blocked out all memories. He deleted the past that he wished he never had. He would never contact the one he loved again. A deep emptiness filled his heart. A void so deep that his body became a lifeless shell. Cold, heartbroken and alone. A man who no one loved. Evan decided to continue his research career and enrolled in an environmental course at the state university.

It was September 2008 when Evan, on his way to his ecology class, caught the eyes of a woman sitting on a park bench with books on her lap. One look into her eyes and he recognised her immediately, love at first sight. This is what he thought. The darkness in his heart only attracted more pain. Each relationship that Evan fell into became a power struggle. Tragedies of emotional pain. With each failed relationship, Evan became more unrepairable. In order to cover up pain, Evan focused on education. Finishing his degree, he began working for an environmental NGO[2]. He conformed to social norms and standards of behaviour. He worked hard to climb the status ladder. That was seven years ago.

With a deep sigh, Evan finished his story. He held Sarah's hand in his and said, 'I would like to forgive myself. I was too busy with career and ambition to look at my broken self. It is the social hierarchies that I have inherited that play out in my relationships. Putting myself and others on pedestals. I don't want to stand tall all the time. I simply created this identity to hide my low self-worth. I forgive myself for I have inherited the harmful dysfunctions of the society that I never questioned, because I was yet to think for myself. I was told that knowledge is power. Yet, knowledge is simply power over others as long as we are possessed by it. We cannot think for ourselves if we are not free. By carrying the entity of hurt, I inevitably triggered this entity in others. I forgive myself because I do not wish to carry the feelings of hurt and pain all the way to my deathbed. I forgive myself so that I can love, not because I owe something to someone but because I have psychologically freed myself from motive. From the psychological cords that create emotional dependence. I do not wish to blame anyone for the tragedies in my life. There is no need for apology nor regret. I have seen many of my friends crumble, trying to work with the effigies that society

2 Non government organisation

fits them into. This society is the source of diseases of the mind and body. It profits from our dependence on medication and chasing our shadows.

'I thank the woman who I may never see again. She broke the identities I had inherited from society: the identity of hierarchy and the ladder leading to the so-called top. I forgive the past to heal my wounds.' With this, Evan relaxed and lowered his eyes.

Sarah gave Evan a warm hug. 'I too am learning the language of love,' she said. 'We each find our own way to light the flame in our heart. It is this light at the bottom of the well that is the eternal flame of love. As long as this flame burns, we are never alone. I love you Evan.'

Sarah kissed Evan goodnight and walked out into the winter night. A smile spread over her face as she thought, 'We are attracted to each other to expose all that prevents us from loving ourselves.'

★ ★ ★

To forgive is to honour those who blessed us with the transformative agent of pain. When emotional pain becomes unbearable, it breaks the threshold of what the mind can withstand. When we have no choice but to give up and completely surrender, we are blessed with the miracle of freedom. This freedom is ours because it was "For-Given". We forgive because we value our own self-worth. This is how much we honour ourselves. We forgive the past for we cannot reverse the arrow of time. We forgive the curse of the future for it deprives us of the miracle that is this moment. The destination we seek is always this moment; it releases us from the psychological chords trapped in the memories of time. The ladder of success no longer keeps us running away from what is sacred. Forgiveness transforms a victim by giving them the strength of vulnerability. We can return with love to places that once held memories of tragedy. Forgiveness is realising that there is nothing to forgive.

Strength of Vulnerability

There is a space
that exists within us
around us
it surrounds us
where angels sing
on rays of light
and love was born
in the heart of the universe

~ Peter Kater and Snatam Kaur

Because we are not perfect, we honour the gift of vulnerability. A tree has no concept of perfection. It simply grows in the direction of the light. The act of growth gives air to those who breathe, shelter to creatures that climb, and nutrients that circulate back to the soil. The eagle hovers over its prey. The rabbit colony below is aware of its presence yet remains impervious to its attack. Nature knows that if all predators were perfect, one day they would run out of prey. Nothing is immune to survival. The bat lets go of sight to hunt in the dark. The moth gains 'ears' and evasive manoeuvres to avoid capture. The arms race of hunter and hunted, the co-evolution of life after dark. Without the uniqueness of each individual, the politician would have to bake his own bread. The merchant would be without goods to sell if there weren't ships to travel the seas. Each individual is cherished for the prosperity of the land.

Yet we are afraid of being seen. Fear grips us because who we are cannot be explained or defined by society. Our most elaborate explanations are mere remnants of poetry giving feeling to contemplation. Who are we to break the limits of perception, to break all identity and become the unknown? Without this timeless dimension, we feel a great lack, because no amount of identity can match this magnificence. No matter how many identities we have, no matter how many hats we wear, there is nothing as powerful as who we truly are. So we add more to ourselves. We add more perfection to illusion. We add aesthetic beauty, money, career and relationships to substitute our own magnificence. When this lack intensifies, we numb it with food, sex, drugs and alcohol. Perfection becomes a perpetual state of non-acceptance of who we truly are. The more we cover ourselves up, the less we want to be seen. In fact, it is when we strive for perfection that we become pretentious. No one has ever found a flaw in imperfection.

Take the woodworker who does not sing in front of his companions for fear of their friendly insults. He convinces himself that his customers need his furniture. That singing is for those who have been gifted this talent. He abandons the opportunity to practice in fear of annoying the passersby with his noise. Hiding his yearnings, a part of him withdraws from all aspects of his life. Making furniture becomes a mindless routine lacking the passion he once had for it. Making love becomes a non-committal pleasure for he cannot fully see himself. Not yet. Not until he removes the illusion that guards his heart. He avoids anything that provokes deeper meaning for if he were to commit, it would expose the self from which he is hiding.

Next door, the young woman with her fragrant products and healing potions is always energetic. She is talkative and overly friendly. She is constantly engaging people and finding ways to connect. Silence is what makes her uncomfortable. Silence would mean facing her fears so tonight she will go out to dance. Tomorrow she has scheduled meetings with her clients. Then, she will update her stocks. She has even scheduled some rest. She will go for a walk on the beach where the young men play volleyball. She always has something to do so that she is seen as pleasing and productive. Yet, she too is running from herself. She does not know who she is because she creates her personality to please those who are around her. She is impatient and speaks of many things all at once. She is easily disappointed because she wants to be part of everything, yet it is not these things that interest her, it is the need to be noticed. She is constantly complimenting those around her in order to seek their approval, to feel loved and appreciated. Yet to find love in herself would mean facing the pain that has created a fortress around her heart. Unfortunately the fortress can only be opened from within. No amount of approval will ever awaken love in her heart.

It is therefore an act of enormous courage to be seen in our vulnerability.

In order to be vulnerable we accept all parts of ourselves as neither good nor bad. This frees judgment from the eyes of the observer. In our vulnerability we become the embodiment of truth. Vulnerability has nothing to do with exposing the horrors we accumulated when we faced the dark. There is a difference between being a victim and being vulnerable. The entity within the victim has a strategy to attract attention from a story of misfortune. The state of deprivation is incredibly unattractive yet the victim is absorbed in the depths of their drama, constantly seeking a willing ear. When the victim is unsuccessful at pulling people into their story, they attack the listener so that they too can be hurt. The entity within the victim wants someone else to feel their pain. To be vulnerable is an enormous act of courage because it requires us to let go of what we love the most: the story that gives our life meaning. We are then able to share our story without draining the ones who have so kindly offered their presence. We can share the story of a victim with the freedom of forgiveness. Those blessed to hear such a story would welcome vulnerability with open arms and hearts ready to offer.

The Untold - Story of relinquishing psychological scars

This was a story she would die without telling. This is what she had once told herself. Now, as she stood in front of an intimate audience of 35 people, the vow of silence broken; her story to be shared with strangers and friends alike.

She lived in Rio De Janeiro, Brazil and at 22, she was in no hurry to find a husband. Men, all they wanted was sex and she was an attractive woman. She knew how to talk men into having sex and how to shut them off from coming on to her. She was outgoing and spent her nights out dancing in Lapa where the best night clubs are. Sometimes, she let the foreigners drop her home, leaving them on her doorstep. She knew they would be back with gimmicks of romance which she would kindly accept. She would allow them to have her body but not her heart. She preferred to sleep with foreign men because they would eventually leave Rio, to go back to their countries, back to their jobs and sometimes back to their wives.

She preferred the company of men. In the presence of other women, she felt competitive. But it was not men nor women that she was afraid of, it was herself. She had spent countless nights in tears because no matter how many men she slept with, she could never allow herself to feel loved. Men would pound her hard in bed because they could not feel her love. She would leave them exhausted because no matter how much they gave, her heart was not yet open to receiving them. Her heart had been locked shut by guilt and shame. Guilt that she was the victim and the one who had committed the crime; shame that she could not reach out for support. Back then, she was 15 and she hid the tears from her family. She would lock her room and enter the great land of sorrow where tears turn into rivers that overwhelm its banks, and continue to flow even when she has forgotten what she was crying about. For it is not that night that haunts her any more, it is the residue of the foul act that decays her body. The act that has made her uncomfortable in her own skin. Such is the distance from her heart that she is unable to feel the twisted pleasure that comes from pain. From the men who turn up at her doorstep with leather and locks. So hidden is her silence that she has forgotten what pain feels like. At least in her late teens, she could feel. Now though, no one notices.

Why does she go out each night?

'She loves to dance'

Why is she always with men?

'She's attractive'

Why doesn't she stay with men?

'They are foreigners'

Tonight though, she is going to make up for seven years of silence. Trembling with the trauma that she is about to share, she looks at her audience. She sees some of her friends from childhood. She's been out for dinner with them occasionally and seen them at birthday parties. She realises that by keeping silent, she has robbed herself of true friendships. It does not matter now. One of the foreigners whom she had not slept with had encouraged her to attend this event: Authentic Storytelling. She'd decided that if she were to learn anything about authenticity, she'd learn by doing it rather than experiencing it second-hand. And now is the moment to speak.

'I was 15. It was an overcast night and the stars were not visible. I was walking through Rocinha[3] with an older boy whom I had met once before at school. He had attempted to kiss me twice that evening and I had refused but he was annoyingly persistent and I was waiting for him to lose interest in me.

'Suddenly, the boy pulls me into a narrow alley. Before my instinct kicks in, he hits me sharply on my head with something hidden in his hand. When I wake up, it feels like my body has been repeatedly hammered against a wall. True, I have been raped. But as time goes on it is not so much the rape that hurts me as not being able to speak about it. Ashamed, I did not know who to turn to. For the first five years, I cried until I had forgotten the reason for tears. And the tears still came. I felt filthy in my own body. My friends had long deserted me, as if they had picked up on the stench of my defiled body. Two years ago, a foreign man started flirting with me on Ipanema beach. I had not been seen in this way for years but I craved company and we slept together that night. From that moment on, I started making an effort to look beautiful. I would go to the night clubs at Lapa to seduce men, not to sleep with them but to know that I could control them. I was the predator and they were the prey. Men are so easily manipulated. Sexually frustrated, they were helpless in the restlessness of the night.'

'But it is not the approval of men that I want anymore. I want the approval of myself. To love my own body. For my scars to heal. I don't think I will ever be ready but I want to move on. To move past the story I have never told. I have no one left to blame. I want to let go of the guilt.

3 Rocinha is the largest Favela (slum) in Brazil

The shame. I want to be seen for what happened and be forgiven for it. I want to be seen as beautiful from within. To have the healing rain wash away the toxic residues that still circulate all over my body. I want to be heard because this is the one thing that I don't have words for. I can't even feel pain anymore. I want to be loved! I want to be loved! I want to be loved by the person who I'm unable to look at in the mirror.'

With this, she closes her eyes and tears start to flow. They shimmer softly down her cheeks as she stands in front of friends and strangers alike. No one says a word. The silence, deafening. She is now too afraid to open her eyes. Tears flowing like rivers again; feelings returning to her skin. She relives the experience she had seven years ago. That overcast night when she was lead into the alley. Back to where it began. She is alone again. She is going to pick herself up. She is going to ask for support. She is no victim of a tasteless crime. She is a child created through an act of love and she will shine her light once again! She opens her eyes. No one is seated anymore. They all surround her arm in arm ready to engulf her in love. She falls into their arms like a child curling up into the arms of their mother.

★ ★ ★

Vulnerability has a beauty seen by many who cannot take that step for themselves. Perfections and imperfections are illusions of the mind. And once this is recognised, the mind can conclude its affair with labels and finally see that *this is it*. Vulnerability is to look into the eyes of another and remind them of their own magnificence. To see that there is nothing more to add. There is absolutely nothing impure about the light that sees neither the good nor the bad, but breaks through these facades to reach directly to the heart. Vulnerability is the pathway to purity. To authenticity. Vulnerability moves past the standards of behaviour that disguises the feelings we so politely hide. Only through vulnerability are we able to share our deepest longings and only though vulnerability are they instantly received as truth.

Embodiment of Truth

Blessed we are to dance on this ground, the rhythm of saints to carry the sound. We pray for the earth, for the ones yet to come, may you walk in beauty
and remember your song.

~ Peia Luzzi

Why is it so difficult to speak Truth? To say what we think. To share our heart's desire. Perhaps we have given up. Perhaps we think there is no point. Things will always be the same. Perhaps Truth takes too much effort. Perhaps it's easier to live a lie because everyone else is doing the same and we do not wish to be alone. Perhaps speaking truthfully will hurt someone we hold dear. Perhaps speaking truthfully would mean letting go of a part of ourselves that we have become familiar with; a part of ourselves we crave out of habit. One that we maintain because this is how we relate to those around us. Perhaps by speaking Truth, we may destroy the relationships that we have built over many years. Perhaps speaking Truth would mean losing everything we know.

The son returns home. He had been gone so long that they thought he was never coming back. The mother does not ask of his journey. Words are too overwhelming in the face of his presence. She simply goes to the kitchen to prepare him a meal. This is how she will show her love. The father sits with him on the couch. He is glad that his son is home. He would like him to stay and settle. Even though he too has travelled the world and seen many things. He tells his son that his room is upstairs and he can stay with them for as long as he needs. The son has experienced many things that conflict with the conservative nature of his family. Yet no amount of talking will shift the harmony that suffocates his family. What is the point of fixing something that is not broken? This is what he thinks. During breakfast the next morning, the mother says to her son, 'You look sad. Are you not happy to see us?' The son wants to leave again even though he longs for their company. He says, 'I'm not looking forward to going back to work. The mother is happy that her son is already thinking about a job.'

It is much easier to live the illusion than to shatter all that we know. All is well. Why look for deeper meaning? Gone are the days when we went in search of wise men and medicine women who spoke words that gave meaning to our existence. The gift of knowledge was held by the few who walked the path of discovery. Today wisdom is delivered to us as daily tweets. We live in a world where too few think before speaking, and too many speak without thinking. There are those who use the mind to explain, who believe science gives reasons for our existence and dismiss that which cannot be explained. Theirs is the perception that is capped by rationality.

Then there are others who become witnesses to the activities of the mind; the observers of duality, striving towards equanimity. They have read the scriptures passed down by ancient lineages. They have done ceremony in distant lands that still believe in God and do not question the integrity of the tradition handed down to them over generations. They talk about being grateful, about mindfulness and compassion. They devote themselves to gurus, teachers and other such curators of ancient knowledge. They place God on a pedestal; an external entity of supreme power that demands their faith.

And there are others who are not satisfied with what they have been told to believe and search in despair for the meaning of it all. They get lost in the detail and then realise that the mind can reach a point of saturation. Then they awaken within, and see that the mind is not the source of knowledge, but that which makes it visible. They see that knowledge is a spell that blinds us from the truth. They face the terrible fate of letting go of all that they know.

The mind is a servant. Until the spell is broken, the mind continues to serve illusion. Pain, fear and anger: illusions of emotion. Money, power and greed: illusions of destination. Even acts of kindness, appreciation and gratitude fall short when reasoned through the mind. To remind ourselves to be grateful is a tragic mistake. Gratitude comes when the heart is overwhelmed with love. The heart needs no reminding of what it already is. Only the mind needs reasons. When we speak the opinions of the mind, we have departed from the truth. The truth is singular. All else is illusion. It is illusion that needs convincing. It is illusion that needs defending. It is illusion that is exorbitant.

Ascension beyond the mind ends duality altogether. Duality exists as the conflict between the mind and the heart. When we are possessed by the mind, we cannot access the intelligence of the heart. The mind will weigh up possibilities, assess risks and rewards and consider the value of what it invests its attention into. The mind will defend what it thinks. But we are not concerned here with the attention the mind demands. We do not tell our heart what to do, we listen to what it has to say. The heart is consumed by love, and therefore feels no conflict of emotion. The heart does not consider itself separate from all else and therefore by serving itself, it serves all. We choose heart over mind despite the uncertainty, for no amount of planning will ever prepare us for the unknown. We choose heart over mind despite the fear, for it is fear that keeps us trapped in the illusion of security. Death is a certainty, no matter how carefully we live. We choose heart over mind even though it may go against everything we know for the heart is never mistaken.

The mind is a servant. It serves whatever its attention is directed to. When the attention of the mind is absorbed in thoughts of wealth, career, relationship, heath, family and other aspects of life that demands importance, we enter the realm of duality. The duality that struggles between health and wealth, between career and relationship. Change is inevitable. Everything we turn our attention to will eventually come to an end. It is the end we fear, as the mind loses its grip on the job that we outlive, the relationship that becomes distant, the identity that becomes a stranger. We direct the mind's attention within. Into the heart until the awareness expands to the ends of the universe. Until we merge with eternal consciousness of nothing. The nothing cannot be described, since any attempt makes nothing into something. Yet it is in *nothing* that we find the deepest meaning. Our full attention withdraws from the external and the focal point becomes the internal dimension. We no longer incur the fear of loss. There is nothing left to lose. It is this endless expanse that is the intelligence of the heart. The moment the mind surrenders to an intelligence that is far greater than itself, the conflict between the mind and the heart comes to an end. When the mind is refusing to flee from love, there is no need to believe in ourselves, to prove ourselves or justify our existence. We exist and therefore we are. Truth is spoken without defence.

We are the Embodiment of Truth. We have no concept of what Truth is and therefore we speak with clarity. The clarity that arrives in this moment. The truth that we let go of the moment it is spoken. The truth that is like the wind. We know not where it came from or where it went. Yet it brings our awareness to what is invisible. It is the moment that decides what is spoken. It is the moment that decides whether we be strong or soft.

The Miller's son has an immediate attraction to the young girl with a red flower in her hair. He sees her writing in her journal under the oak tree each day as he walks by the stream to the mill on the other side of the hill. It does not take them long to become fond of each other. Each day from that moment on, the Miller son's heart jumps with delight at her sight. Each day from that moment on, the girl with a red flower looks into his eyes and says, 'I love you'. The Miller son never says 'I love you' back. He thinks that he can only say it when he absolutely means it. She thinks that if she doesn't give up, one day his heart will open. Because we don't leave matters that are important to the heart until they are too late. They both keep to their version of truth but speak nothing of it. A year goes by and she never misses a day to say 'I love you'. There isn't a day that goes by that his heart doesn't skip with delight at her sight. As the days add up, the love in the Miller son's heart begins to compound. Each day brings with it the miracles of the heart. Then one day he wakes up and thinks: love in his heart there will always be, why not expand this vibration of the love beyond himself?

The love in his heart begins to multiply, rapidly. That day as he walks by the stream, he sees the girl with the red flower under the oak tree. She comes running to him. They embrace in an eternal hug and then she looks into his eyes and says 'I love you', just like before. This time, the Miller son is unable to withhold the eruption of love that is within him. His heart explodes and he spills love all over her. The girl with the red flower receives back what she said each day without relent, a million times over.

When we look into our hearts, we may find many things. However, it is the moment that decides what to share now and what may be understood later.

GRAESSLE THE GREAT - STORY OF FALSE SALVATION

Graessle woke up as if he had just been spat out by the ocean. A recluse in the ancient desert of the Kimberley, Western Australia. He had never seen the ocean. He wore the remnants of rags which were once clothes. His withering body ruptured like fissures on the enduring rocks of the outback. To this Graessle lacked concern. He had been alone in the desert for seven years. He, alone! He could do as he pleased. He, the one who set foot on the highest mountain he could see. He, who lay claim to the largest cave of the land. He, the savage who ate any creature that he could find. He, the commander of the kingdom no one else knew of. He, Graessle the Great.

Graessle had an exceptional gift. He could read minds. When Graessle was a boy he was placed in an institution for children with unexplained medical disorders. Graessle had started to speak of the terrible thoughts that were in the heads of the heathen of a family he grew up in. Graessle's mother was a service worker. She would come home exhausted and cursing the staff and patients she worked with. Graessle would read her thoughts and say, 'I wish that old lady would drop dead'. He would vocalize the flood of negativity and foul language that was in his mother's head. Graessle also spoke of the murderous thoughts his dad had for his mum.

His dad was an unemployed alcoholic. His dad would assault his mum for money, food and sex. Graessle would speak out loud the violent thoughts his dad had towards his mum. Graessle's parents, terrified by their son's first words, sent him straight to the institution for rehabilitation. At the institution Graessle was seen by psychiatrist Peter Spooner. Graessle told Spooner of how attractive the young nurse in the opposite room was and all the things that he wanted to do to her. Spooner diagnosed Graessle as a reverse-paedophile and put him in solitary confinement. He was to be administered sedative drugs twice a day because we must sedate what we cannot understand. The solitary chamber did not bother Graessle as he could still hear the thoughts of the psychotic patients in his own head. After three months at the institute, Spooner concluded that Graessle could not be treated and classed him as highly dangerous even though Graessle was yet to act out any of the thoughts he had read from other people's minds.

When Graessle was 14, the district health care shut down the institute, due to lack of funding. Spooner found a new job as the dean of psychiatric research at a nearby children's hospital. Graessle was transferred to the prison for young adults and joined the other dangerous adolescents. The disturbed teenagers at the adolescent prison stayed away from Graessle, for fear of having their own thoughts spoken back to them. Graessle spent eight years in the adolescent prison until one day at the age of 22 he was told he would be transferred to the main prison because of overcrowding and increasing influx of teenage criminals. While he was being escorted to the transfer vehicle, Graessle expressed the violent thoughts of the co-driver towards the young delinquents. The co-driver lost control and beat Graessle to near death. The staff at the prison cast a blind eye on Graessle. Loss of another insignificant life. They left him for dead for the violent crimes that he was yet to commit.

Graessle woke up in a deserted prison in the dead of the night. He walked out of the prison covered in blood. He walked past coal mines and into the desolate desert. He came across a broken pipe from which he licked the water and continued walking deeper into the centre of the Australian outback. One day he found a death adder swallowing a rat. He killed the death adder with a sharp-edged rock and ate both the snake and the rat.

Seven years passed in the sea of sand. It was a cloudless day when Graessle came across some towering limestone cliffs. He looked at the cliffs for a long time. Could this be possible? No human thought had ever touched these limestone walls. He came closer. His was the first footsteps on the base of this great landmark. He climbed all the way to the top and basked in the glory of having climbed the mountain no human ever had. After having indulged in this precious moment, Graessle lay down and fell into a deep sleep. For the first time in Graessle life, he experienced a dream.

In this dream Graessle is in a tiny boat in the middle of a vast ocean. The ocean is calm and the sky clear. Graessle is floating aimlessly and the feeling is quite pleasant. Then suddenly, the waves get bigger, thunder clouds approach and the ocean is engulfed by a ferocious storm. Graessle's little boat capsizes. He clings on to it for dear life, but a 20-foot wave sucks him deep into its watery grave. Graessle surfaces and gasps for air only to be buried by another wave. Before the next swell, he manages to climb onto the rudder of the boat. Then in front of him appears the Angel of the Storm. The Angel is wearing an electric fluorescent gown, her hair long, glittering like the ocean under the moon light. She is visible yet Graessle can see right through her. Graessle cannot read her mind. He panics, not because he cannot hear her thoughts but because of the lack of thought in his own mind. The Angel then speaks softly to Graessle. 'My dear Graessle, how long have I waited for you to speak.' Graessle does not understand what she means. His mind is empty. Thoughtless for the first time! 'Speak to me dear one,' says the Angel. Graessle is frozen speechless. He begins to make noises that sound like coughing. He has no words. He, Graessle who knew everything that anyone had ever thought, has no words. The Angel smiles at him and asks again, 'Speak my sweetheart.' Graessle lets out a cry of anguish and the words automatically fly out of his mouth, 'I Don't Know!' The Angel starts to fade back into the invisible. Graessle desperately reaches out to her and the Angel blesses him with her final words, 'That is the answer.'

Graessle wakes up as if he had just been spat out by the ocean... The experience gone, Graessle cannot re-imagine it. He tries to think in despair, yet his mind remains thoughtless. Graessle is unable to think. It is then, that Graessle realises he is unable to read his own mind. He is unable to create thoughts of his own. Graessle starts to weep. For the first time in seven years he begins to feel alone. He gallops uncontrollably down the mountain and finds his way to the nearest road. For three days he walks along the road, before he finally sees a ute coming towards him, driven by a cattle farmer. The farmer cautiously pulls over. He asks Graessle if he needs help. Graessle is unable to read his mind. The words flow out of his mouth, 'Please sir, water.' The farmer gives him his water reserves, and tells him to jump in the back of his ute. He takes him to the local police station where they are unable to find any of his records. The Police class him as a recovered missing person. Graessle is given a small cabin to stay in. He is also given a can of baked beans and a razor to shave off his now enormous beard. Graessle kindly thanks the police officer and stays in the cabin for one night. The next morning he is taken to the community centre where the locals have gathered to identify the missing person.

'Tell us your name,' asks the cattle farmer's wife.

'Graessle,' he replies.

'How long were you in the desert?' asks a woman who had two kids to feed.

'How long is the day when the sun does not set?' Graessle states. 'We define the cycles of the sun and the moon as time. Of course, the tides come and go, but why segment reality into past, present and future? If time is linear, how does it move forward? It is not time that changes. It is simply that energy is transformed into matter and then returned back to the formless. It is this change that gives us the illusion of time. However, when did this moment begin? When does this moment end?'

He continues, 'Thought segments reality into a series of comprehensible moments. However, this moment exists simultaneously in all locations. There is no such thing as sooner and this moment cannot be any later. When you are speaking to someone across the world, you speak to them in this moment, regardless of the time difference. So much of our lives are spent in realities that only exist in the head. Time is of our own making. When our heart is beating fast and our day is spent running from one thing to another, an entire week may disappear without us noticing a single day. Yet when the heart is calm and our undivided attention is on the moment, it is seen that each leaf is of its own colour, each cloud its own shape and each eye contact a different story. A day may come to an end yet it may feel like an entire week has passed. Like footprints in the sand, time is a moment captured from eternity.'

'What were you doing in the desert?' asks a boy who always wanted to be like his older brother.

'I am and this is,' Graessle says. 'There is nothing that I can do. Nothing in nature needs to be done. I cannot say that I beat my heart. My heart simply beats. The fish does not say, 'I swim in the sea,' it simply swims. We simply respond as nature intended. Doing is a human condition. By doing we have separated ourselves from nature. We have created farms to feed the overpopulated cities. We have created jobs to pay for our existence. We have created infrastructure to domesticate the populous. We are born as prisoners of our own world. Slaves of the governance built before us. Doing is the obsession of a restless mind. Only when the mind is silent do we have true freedom of choice. It may be our choice to see what lies beyond the valley. It may be a choice to be with someone we have affection for. But we do not *do* an adventure, nor do we *do* a conversation. We *are* the adventure. We *are* the conversation. Doing is what separates us from the harmony of creation.'

'You speak exquisite words but we do not scavenge in the desert for a meal to appear. We have rent to pay and the field to water,' says a cattle farmer who is struggling to maintain his farm and feed his family.

'The day will arrive when you are exhausted from paying the bills, but the bills will still come. Because we defeat the heart's desire in order to abandon our dream, only to invest in a job, a wife, a house and two kids because this is what life has appointed for us. We believe that this is our will yet when we get the job, we realise it is not what we wanted. Still we work hard. We have a wife and two beautiful kids to support. They are our reason for living. We have found happiness in the comfort of our home; we have found happiness because money allows us to do the things we dream of. We have found happiness because our children grow up to go to college. Yet with each day that passes, we bury our dream until our dream finally vanishes. Then, the things we thought would make us happy suddenly seem empty. We find there is no way out of all the responsibilities we have accumulated. Each day we find ourselves too busy. Too busy dying. We find that in the struggle to get to the top, we have isolated ourselves from the stranger who sits next to us. We have isolated ourselves from the houses that are around us. We have isolated ourselves from the fire that is the heart of a community. We are then alone with a dwindling heart. After all, it was our desire to go against our heart's will. To abandon our prophecy.

'It is then that we take a chance. We pray to all the gods in existence for a drop of the enthusiasm we once had. We learn that it is the heart's desire to connect us all. To offer ourselves and be of service. To treat the children of our neighbours as if they were our own. To share what we have more of. We are not alone in our struggles. Why then must we face these struggles alone? We open our hearts and realise that we are capable of so much more. We are the ones who light the flame when it gets dark. We are the ones who sing when there are no words left to say. We are the ones who lead when there is no path left to follow. We walk the noble path, reminding each precious human being of their own magnificence.'

'The world is already the way it is. There is nothing we can do about it,' says a widow who is yet to see her grandchildren.

'You are right. The world already is and there is nothing to do. With this we honour this moment. We honour the gift that is life. We give reverence to the ancient lineages that live in our bones. We give reverence to this body that has been through everything we have experienced. We give reverence to the hands that have guided us in times of doubt. The hands that have nurtured us when we felt alone. The hands that supported us when we had lost all hope of our own. With purity in our heart we witness the miracle that has led us to this moment. The miracle that blesses us with this breath. The miracle that is the ground below each step. May we remember that all is perfect. May we remember that life is sacred. How then, do we greet the sun that appears in the morning? How then do we see the flower that expresses its beauty? How then do we hear the song that pours out of the cries of the soul? How then do we feel love that is the gift of the human heart? It is then that we find Hope. Hope comes from seeing someone better than they see themselves. Hope is seeing the truth in each person. When we see each person in their true form, it allows them to accomplish wonders.'

The police officer interjects in the interest of time. The community meeting had not gone as planned. He says Graessle would be a great cult leader but their town already has a church. The officer than asks the community members to disperse. Graessle is asked to leave the town in their peace and to not share his ideas openly as it may upset some people. Graessle takes the road once more. With truth in his heart, his mind is clear. For once, he had spoken his own mind and not been locked up for it.

★ ★ ★

There may be moments when we are alone in speaking Truth. We still speak the Truth. We know no other way, for the mind has forgotten the existence of duality. In these times we do not forget the mind's devotion to the heart. We do not forget the moments of doubt that we face yet we still chose the path of the heart. We do not forget the struggles the mind has overcome in order to surrender to the heart. In these times we honour the hands that have led us. For we do not arrive at love by ourselves. It is through each other that we learn to love ourselves.

PART TWO

Intelligence of the Unknown

This part of the book looks at the practical aspects of accessing the subconscious. Only by shifting our subconscious do we see lasting effects in ourselves. By working with the subconscious we shift our visceral state. It is this visceral reprogramming that is reflected in the vitality of the brain and body.

Honouring the Body

Time is a game
played beautifully
by children.

~ Heraclitus

Blessed are the innocent for theirs are the eyes that sparkle with delight. How is it that we lose our innocence as we get older? How is it that our minds begin to fill with questions that brings us to our knees yet we prefer to keep them unrealised. It is precisely these questions that keep us humble. The noble quest to remain childlike despite how much we know. It is with great joy that a child does that which has no meaning. The abundance of energy makes them bounce as they run towards a tree, swing on a rope, or throw a rock into a lake. The child does not seek benefit from play. Play is the benefit. It is when we play that we are most confident. This is the freedom of discovering instinct: the innate intelligence that gives genuine expression to the body.

Play as I define it is different from games which may be based on competition and where strategy and tactics may be involved. Play differs from games that involve deceit and chance such as gambling. Play as I define it is devoid of agenda and occurs in a time-free space. Play may involve altered consciousness for example, trance or vertigo. Play may also involve mimicry, dance and theatre. Play is clever, in mysterious ways. It is through play that evolution has decided we would learn. We honour our body through play; without it, how can we listen to our body when it has forgotten how to speak.

So we play. We dance unapologetically as the sun sets on a remote beach. We collapse and roll in the sand. We sing and laugh like it's nobody's business. We chase and tackle each other through the autumn forest as our body glides over the ocean of fallen leaves. The joy erupts from our hearts as we express our freedom. All the while, our body is being enriched with information. Stimulated in ways we have not yet experienced. It is when our dance becomes a trance that we really begin to move. The mind forgets all that it has learnt. The body moves without the interruption of thought. The mind bears witness to the elegance of human grace.

The young innovator is too busy to play. He has important work to do; work that will bring sustainability to the land and convenience to the people. His mind saturates each day with ideas, yet he hasn't got the patience to see them through; he is already thinking about his next idea. He doesn't seem to understand why investors are not interested in his ideas. Why his friends avoid him when he speaks of his passion. Investors do not tell him that the ideas have become obsessions of the head and the simplicity of the solution has long been forgotten. His friends find him difficult to talk to because conversations very quickly become serious. The young investor is yet to learn that perhaps it is the matters of grave importance that we must take lightly. The young innovator battles with his head to find a solution to his disconnection, yet no amount of logic will get him out of his head. The young innovator sees kids playing in the park. How unproductive! He is an important man and as such his thoughts shall express sophistication. Yet he fails to realise that in that moment, play may be the best use of his time. To be sure, play is what frees us from the linearity of goal-directed thoughts.

We honour the intelligence of the body—the intelligence that is derived from billions of years of evolutionary selection—through play. This intelligence gave rise to the structure of our bones, the viscosity of our blood, the defence of our immune system, the texture of our skin, the shape of our feet, the articulations of our joints, the flexibility of our spine and the harmony of our organs. This intelligence is enough to keep the body alive. We do not need a big brain. Yet because of our big brains, we have completely bypassed natural selection.

We no longer live as our ancestors did, with direct communion of all our senses with the sun and the moon and the cycles of the land. We no longer have the natural systems regulating our populations such as disease, predator-prey relationships and natural phenomena such as drought. Without these natural agents to keep us in harmony, we now live in a paradox. We think we are the dominant species on this planet. Yet, the success of one species is impossible in nature. Isolating ourselves from the intricate balance of all things, we have engineered ourselves into a monoculture. The human species itself is critically endangered. There is only a handful of us left in the wild, some in the Highlands of Papua New Guinea and some in the rainforest of the Amazon. Other than this, there are no wild human populations left in existence. We are a species raised in captivity. What is the cost of this captivity?

The cost of captivity is evident in our bodies and our brains. The evolution of humankind has become so distant to that of nature. The education system is responsible for mass disembodiment. By the time our children leave the education system, they have become chronic thinkers. Educated out of our bodies, we can no longer hear it speak. Our bodies stopped speaking to us when we decided that we knew better and began to design our own nature. In doing so, we have created real problems to drive out imaginary ones. We have created infrastructure that has cost us our natural mobility and has progressively disabled us. We do not need to look far to see evidence of disconnection, we shall find it in our daily breath.

Breath

Our first in-breath gives birth to life. Our last breath out takes it away. The life that we know is the journey between these two breaths. In our mind-driven world, breathing has been overlooked as a necessary activity. Without breath, there is no life. So intricately linked is breath with all else that occurs within the body that we cannot deny we are at the mercy of our own breath.

The sole pump of the body is the heart. Our heart rate varies with each breath. Each time we inhale, the heart rate[4] rises and each time we exhale, it slows down. Many cultures have capitalised on this natural process to develop a multitude of breathing techniques. I describe here a technique of my own making, vagal breathing. To inhale through the nose and exhale without force, through the mouth. During the inhalation, we become aware of all that is around us. We notice everything. We use the exhale to relax the body. The exhalation relaxes the heart and therefore the rest of the nervous system. As such we keep the exhalation twice as long as the inhalation. Because the heart rate governs the physiological processes of the brain and body, I consider the heart to regulate the central nervous system (CNS), unlike the conventional understanding of the brain as the command centre.

The purpose of breathing in is to become aware; the purpose of exhaling to relax the body.

Breathing can be clavicle. In this case we take short, shallow breaths; a form of hyperventilation. This form of breathing is useful when the body is in panic. The first response of the nervous system, when we go into fight or flight mode (sympathetic activation), is to hold the breath in. To resist the flow of breath is to resist the flow of life. So in instances of panic we continue to breathe until we are able to slow down breath into deep inhalations and slow exhalations.

Breathing can be diaphragmatic. This is where we breathe deep into the lungs. The diaphragm expands on the in-breath and relaxes on the out-breath. This is our daily breath. The breath that we accompany as we walk through a city park or wait in a queue. The breath we accompany as we go about our habits and behaviours.

Breathing can be abdominal. The belly rises when we breathe in and contracts when breathing out. This form of breathing induces deep relaxation. This is the breath we use when we sit in meditation. This meditation is body-based and travels the internal landscape. With eyes

---

4 The heart rate variability (HRV) due to breathing is known as Respiratory Sinus Arrhythmia

closed, the inhalation observes the sensations of the body. The exhalation relaxes the body. As the awareness of the breath grows, we recognise tightness in various parts of the body, perhaps in the neck or the adductors of the hips? Deep breathing releases the body of hypertonicity - chronic tension held by the nervous system.

Once this mechanism becomes innate, our body will naturally rely on these breathing techniques without our guidance. We then become aware of the difference between moving with our breath and using our breath to move. When we move with the breath, we are synchronising our breathing with whatever activity our body is doing. I would emphasise that breath is primary and movement is secondary. In this case we use the breath to relax the body. When movement is initiated through breath, the quality of our movement changes. Movement is a relationship between tension and relaxation of the muscles. Through breath, we remove unnecessary tension from the muscles for our movements to become clean and efficient. Our movements become less corrosive. Movement becomes a medium to heal the body. Because breath is primary, we use our breath to move. Regardless of the intensity of the movement, we are able to regulate our breath and keep our body selectively relaxed.

Breath. Relaxation. Movement. This is the fail-proof kinetic chain. The pathway[5] to healing the body.

Healing our Senses

Our senses have been possessed by comforts and attractions that lure the mind. So deep are these obsessions that we become dependent on our senses. It is this deep disconnection from our own body that creates sensory deprivation and therefore the addiction to stimulation.

5 The fundamental pathway is derived from the Russian Technique known as *Systema.*

Touch

The affection with which a mother makes first contact with her newborn, the release of oxytocins, the nurturing of the most pervasive bond in nature, love; it is this sense of touch that we crave for. Yet, when love is not saturated in our hearts, our touch lacks this natural affection. Touch does not lie. The body is able to viscerally sense intention. So instead of nurturing love in our hearts, we have forbidden the gift of touch. We have prohibited the gift of touch from our schools, from our work places and social activities. Touch has become sexualised and it is through intimacy that we now discover the ecstasy of sensation. However, the sense of touch is short-lived, even in intimacy. Without full awareness of the largest organ of our body, the skin, we have forgotten that touch has the capacity to heal or to harm. When we touch someone with anger, it leaves an emotional imprint that is far deeper than any visual scar. The strength of the touch does not matter. That is to say, anger is transmitted viscerally no matter how subtle the touch, so too can we can hit someone and heal them.

The Russian military training known as Systema uses physical strikes to induce relaxation in the aggressor. A relaxed strike penetrates deeper into the tissue and organs than a strike that is tense with aggression. The act of striking someone with a relaxed fist can momentarily cause blackout. The sudden blackout neutralises the nervous system. Once the aggressor regains consciousness, they have to re-imagine the scenario that instigated their aggressive motives. Relaxed strikes quite often trigger uncontrollable laugher. It is through these involuntary hysterics that the body releases deep rooted trauma. It is through the sense of touch that we learn about our visceral sensations, the hydraulics of the fluid that circulates in our bodies and the movement of our organs.

Touch is what grounds us in this body. The ability to feel our feet in contact with the primary surface, the ground we stand on. Without the sensation of the primary contact we are psychologically less grounded in ourselves. The foot has 26 bones, connected by 33 joints. When we insulate our feet from making contact with the ground, these joints are deprived from stimulation and begin to fuse. High-heeled shoes alter foot structure obscenely. Our feet have an intelligence similar to that of our hands. When our hand reaches for a cup, it automatically acquires the shape it needs to fit the cup. Likewise, the hand moulds its shape to that of a door knob. Feet also have this intelligence and can map the surface of the terrain as we wander. Not only have we insulated our feet, we have also smoothed the surface we walk on. Like our bones, nothing in nature is linear. When we walk in the forest, our bare feet experience the reflexology of nature. The feet make contact with smooth pebbles, perching roots, slippery leaves and angles of all kinds. We relax the foot when it makes contact with the ground to allow it to mould onto the surface of the terrain. In an age where we are so focused on the next step, we forget the step we are taking now. So we walk to embody our sole.

Because of our distant relationship with our primary contact, we have saturated our sensations to our hands and have lost sensitivity with the rest of the body. The relationship a contemporary dancer has with the ground is enriched with twists, turns, rolls, inversions, spins and slides. Our limbs change our relationship with gravity, yet when our body is fully supported by the primary surface, we are able to nurture all the surfaces of our skin. The skin craves this contact; the heightened sensitivity that comes through relaxation awakens the instinct of the skin, known as body schema, the relationship of the body with space. It is our body schema that defines our comfort zone or the length of our limbs which may expand when we hold a walking stick. It is through schema enrichment that we discover the gift of touch.

Temperature

The skin is temperature-sensitive. Our temperature-regulated lifestyles displace the natural mechanisms of the body to regulate our temperature.

We have the luxury of heated showers and air conditioned rooms. We then begin to fear the cold and become averse to heat. Neither extreme is beneficial for extended periods however there exists a difference between actual temperature and psychological temperature. Despite the cold, we are able to physiologically generate heat. In the manner described in the breathing section above we can use breath to increase our metabolic rate and therefore our heat production. As a general rule, the exhalation is twice as long as the inhalation. Equipped with this vagal breathing technique we are able to rely on breath to regulate temperature rather than fall prey to the intolerance of the mind. The ancient Cossacks of Siberia (where Systema originated) follow one such practice that builds tolerances to thermal fluctuations by dousing the body with two buckets of cold water each morning. Cold is a humbling force. The act of cold water dousing is as much a mental practice as it is a physical one. The practice reinforces the trust in the breath rather than the evasive tendencies of the mind. Cold water activates the mammalian dive reflex that drops the heart rate and instantly relaxes the nervous system. This is another way in which the nervous system can be neutralised similar to the blackout that happens when relaxation is induced through a physical hit.

Pain

The relationship to pain may also be redefined. The mentality of *no pain, no gain* is corrosive on the body. When we apply our exhausted minds, rushed by the ever increasing demands of a 'doing based lifestyle', to the body, we are simply complimenting our mental burnout with physically. The body is pushed beyond its means by a self-destructive mindset or a mindset that is addicted to performance. The *no pain, no gain* mindset does more harm than good, but we must not become soft and avert pain either. Many mental strategies capsize when confronted with pain. However deep our denials, we confess with foolish honesty when inflicted with pain.

Once again, it is breath that overcomes the intolerance to pain. When we are focused on breath, we withdraw our attention from pain and from the mental dialogues that accompany it. It is pain that traps people in their heads and gradually renders their bodies inaccessible. It is therefore pain that is the most powerful agent for surrender. It is pain the breaks the mind and instils awareness of the body. When we break past our pain barrier we often experience a state of tranquil euphoria. It is then that our relationship with pain is transformed, the mind a harmless witness to the experience.

The body requires a certain degree of pain and abrasion to strengthen the skin from tear. We strengthen the joints progressively beyond the habitual ranges of motion so that the nervous system learns to relax in ranges it would otherwise struggle, in fear of overexertion. Becoming comfortable with pain makes flexibility practices pleasurable. Our relationship with emotional pain is also transformed. We no longer fear pain, nor do we welcome pain; we are able to fully feel pain as we do joy. It is because we suppress pain that we deny feeling the full spectrum of emotions. Emotions are like clouds that appear in the clear blue sky. We must not deny that they are there. We must not hold on in fear that they may pass. We must not change the emotion that we feel. When we feel anger, we must feel it as we do pain, without the mental dialogues that accompany it. So do we feel excitement and lust without the mental agenda. In this manner our emotions are pure, true to the moment. As the emotion passes, we return back to the clear blue sky. The purity where the energy of emotion is unable to become an entity that accumulates in the body. Holding on to emotions is like holding on to a glass of water. The glass gets heavier the longer we hold it. To be free to feel the full spectrum of emotions is to honour the gift of sensation.

Smell

The sense of smell is ever-present. We drink in the olfactory landscape because we do not have a choice. Yet we are oblivious to this odorous map as we are impervious to the sensations of the clothes that we wear.

So underdeveloped is our sense of smell that we do not yet have the vocabulary to represent smell. When we smell smoke, we do not define it by the details we smell. Is it smoke from wood? Is the wood dry, wet, soft, hard, young, rotting, pine, elm, rose or oak? The formless air is an ever-changing mixture, anew with each breath. It is smell that gives the first premonition into the edibility of what we find in nature. It is smell that gives us an indication of whether a fruit is raw, ripe or rotten. It is this time signature that gives us the capacity to trace scent when sight and sound have long vanished. We no longer use smell to trace edible plants or track prey but instead live in a world seduced by it. The illustrious scent signatures are what guides us to a French bakery before we are aware that we crave a croissant. When smell loosens its intoxicating grip, we become receptive to smells we did not notice before: the smell of dry straw, of a butterfly, of a table cloth or a hummingbird's nest. Sensitivity of smell, like the instinct of touch, can be developed. We look at the acute refinement of a wine connoisseur, the delicate fragrance conjured by a perfumer or the subtle essence combined by an aromatic chef. Smell is a sensation not to be discarded by the mind but felt viscerally. Lush is the world of smell with no apparent lack of odours to discover.

TASTE

The sense of taste is ironic. It is precisely those things that pleasure us that are the most destructive. Our tastebuds are linked to the most primal of our instincts; the gut instinct. Yet this instinct has been hijacked by nutrient-deprived foods. It is the pervasiveness of sugar that has distorted our relationship to food and turned it into one of craving. There is a difference between feeling hungry and being hungry. An empty stomach does not mean that the body needs food. The luxury of food means that we eat for the pleasure rather than the necessity to eat. Yet there is nothing wrong with the pleasure of eating. But rather, we find appreciation in the sensations of food and meditate on the process of chewing. It is then that we realise the quality of what we place in our mouths. Are we tasting the perfection of nature's creation? The fruits of nature are already complete in its taste. Do we pick the berry that grows wild amongst the leaf litter of the forest floor? Or do we devour artificially engineered products that are more pesticide than nutrient? Are we a captive population eating our way to death or is food thy medicine? We eat at the pace at which the food is prepared. How mindlessly are fast foods consumed?

When we prepare our meal ourselves, we pick up the sweet potato and taste it with your hands, smell the rosemary with our gut and then combine the ingredients with all our heart. It is then that we experience the true pleasure of taste. It is then that the body is fed with unspeakable appreciation. True pleasures of taste bring tears to the eyes.

SOUND

The sense of sound speaks to us subconsciously. Sound is encrypted with a wonderment of codes. Frequencies are emitted from different dimensions of consciousness. It is sound that frees us from our internal sense of control. It is sound that causes our body to react with joy, grief or nostalgia. To sound we move, to sound we quiver and surrender. Sound is the voice of our mother. It is the laughter of our lover. It is the expression of the universe through our voice. It is sound that we turn to when we crumble with a broken heart. It is the sacred sounds that heal our hearts. Yet the purity of sound has been hijacked by the media. The media that bombards our consciousness with longings, convinces us of needs, inflates the ego and instils fear. It is sound that has subconsciously clouded our heads with toxic noise. The frequencies of the mind is scattered into many voices, voices that becomes possessive entities. All of nature does not speak at once. Creatures select their time of the day to speak. Likewise, we are unable to disentangle frequencies from multiple conversations. The mind always selects the frequency it decides to listen to. In this manner we can internally select the frequency of our own thoughts. Do the sounds we listen to speak to the entities of the subconscious or do they connect us to a deeper part of ourselves? It is sound that gives a voice to Truth. It is sound that sings of the love radiating from our hearts. Let us cleanse the sounds that enter our ears. For it is sound that alters our consciousness.

Sight

The sense of sight allows us to see ourselves in the mirror. To see what is written on our body. As we form images of ourselves, so too do we form images of those we know or don't. Like the pollution of smell and the noise of sound, we dilute our sight to see only what we are interested in. Our sight selects only that which it perceives as relevant to us. And so we live in a world that demands our attention. Because we have been distorted in our perception of beauty, we seek pleasure from media devices that capture our attention for hours on end. Our visual focus becomes limited to less than half a meter in front of us. Those devices that are on day and night betray us of our night vision and as a result, of our peripheral[6] vision. They have become the antidote to our distracted minds.

We talk and walk without looking at each other or what is around us. Such is our dependence on sight that we hardly see a thing. Eyes are the only visible structure of the brain and thus a direct reflection of our intentions. To truly see is when our attention is focused on nothing. To see nothing frees our attention from the traps of the visible. In this manner we see the world. We see the space between the leaves of a tree. We see that each individual leaf sways differently to the wind. We see the gentle dance of a leaf as it descends to the forest floor. We see the different shades of the leaves as they vanish from existence. When we begin to see, beauty is no

6 Night and peripheral vision are captured by the same set of cells known as rod cells of the retina. Color and acute focus are from cones cells of the retina.

longer hidden from our eyes but is all around us. Beauty is in feeling the emptiness of each object, plant and creature. Beauty is the moment when we look deep into the eyes of another. Beauty is when we penetrate the heart of the one in front of us with the love that radiates from our eyes. It is in the eyes of another that we see the true reflection of our own beauty.

Healing our Movement

Movement is the language of the body. It is our primary language. Speech comes secondary. When we move, we access the intelligence of hundreds of millions of years of evolution that have shaped the body we live in now. This intelligence has been lost almost entirely because we no longer think viscerally. The body intelligence is the trust that we develop in our own skin as kids. We discover our bodies through play. Our bodies are drawn towards the playground where we climb the ladder to slide down. We do this time and time again for the thrill, all the while the body learns to trust its own motion. We think in the language of movement. We run to the swings in the playground. When we kick off the ground to swing, our body has already mapped the way it will sway to generate momentum in the swing. The body does this instinctively. Likewise when we learn to ride a bike, we simply practice. We do not read a manual on how to ride a bike. The thrill and joy of thinking viscerally is very quickly displaced by technique and conditioning that is inherent in sports. We are further displaced from the body as the education system demands that children sit still for hours on end and pay attention to academic subjects. Kids who are unable to comply, whose bodies crave movement and the freedom to explore and discover things for themselves, are medicated and sedated in order to absorb what we think is best for them. The intelligence of the body is overwritten by the overdevelopment of our chronically thinking minds.

A young woman who burnt out from her cooperate job twice in the last three months decides to nurture herself. She goes to a yoga class. She does various sequences of postures and finds herself withdrawing from the hysterics of the mind. Hang on, she must stay focused on her work! No she is making excuses again. She needs something to keep her body on track and her health in check. She will work harder at the postures. The yoga teacher sees herself in the young woman. She also burnt out from her corporate job and got attracted to the idea of relieving stress from the workplace. Yet with her newly acquired identity as a yoga teacher, she finds herself teaching back to back classes to cover costs of rates that are half her weekly wage. She had more financial freedom in her corporate job. Still, it is the romanticised lifestyle that attracts her. She has seen 'celebrity' yoga teachers travel the world sharing what they love. She can still make it. She finds herself in glamorous photo shoots promoting yoga in the competitive fitness market. Yoga, it seems, is more about how her glutes look in the fashionable leggings than the traditional sutras that she learnt in her training course. Trapped in a new identity, she once again finds herself used by an industry. At the end of the class, the young woman approaches the teacher. She too wants to become a yoga teacher. The teacher talks to her of departing from the yoga philosophy and teaching from her mind because she is yet to find her spirit. She talks of the traditions that she makes up on the spot because Sanskrit is a language we all know of. She talks of a time when yoga had rescued her from her demons. It was yoga that she returned to when she considered giving up on her day. It was her practice that kept her steady. Yet, the more she learns about yoga, the less she knows about herself. The young woman listens to the yoga teacher. She is aware that there are many paths to connect with the body and that she is merely attracted to the current trends in vanity.

Is it the prevailing industries that govern the evolution of human movement or is there something far more fundamental?

Movement has become a mindless activity precisely because it is through the mind that we move the body. 'The mind is a beautiful servant but a dangerous master'[7]. The servant has become misguided by it's own self-centric beliefs and resulted in mass disembodiment[8]. Disconnected from our bodies, we no longer trust its intuition and instincts; which remains largely unfamiliar. We then pay the price through the ever growing list of mental and physical diseases. Diseases merely reflect the lack of self-love as the brain struggles to find harmony in the body. Self-love begins with honouring your own body. After all, your body has been with you through every single one of your experiences and will stay with you until the very end. This body that you recognise as an expression of yourself. Your body has a heart that does not stop beating because one day it woke up tired. Until the moment arrives, when you take your last breath and realise that this body, your body, is who you are.

This body is the only asset that is truly yours. Without it, we do not exist. So before all else, we honour this body. We honour its instincts, its aliveness and its wildness. We honour this body with what it desires the most: Breath. It is through breath that we *embody*. It is breath that allows us to access our subconscious intelligence. Through exhaling for at least twice as long as we inhale, we maintain relaxation in the body regardless of the activity we are doing. It is this relaxation that gives us access to what I call 'Visceral Intelligence'.

We do not need to be aware of our movements to move better. It is quite the contrary. We pay attention to breath and relaxation. Breath is primary and so we use the breath to move. 'Movement is simply breath made visible'[9]. By relaxing the body in our everyday movements, we find that our movements acquire a different quality. A flow that was once absent now transpires even in the most mundane of movements. Even when we open the fridge door, there can be a certain grace to our movements. When we reach for the bottom shelf, our body finds an ease that was not

7 Quote by Osho

8 Disembodiment is the lack of brain-body coherence as measured by heart rate variability (HRV)

9 Quote by Anna Halprin

there before. By keeping the attention on the breath, we begin to expose the corrosiveness that is in movement when it is driven mindlessly by habit. The body naturally tends towards efficiency. This is clearly seen when we learn to drive a car, our movements streamline over time. However, this elegance is available not only to learnt movement but is fundamentally the intelligence that drives the body in any activity. Each motion then becomes a joy. When fascination returns to mundane activities, the body is childlike once more. We fall in love with play and suddenly feel young again.

We find the benefits of breath even greater in movements that put stress on the body. For example, body/weight exercises when done through breath and relaxation use far less effort. Take the simple act of getting up from the floor. This movement does not need strength nor momentum. When we use our breath to move, we first initiate a smooth breathing rate, we keep our breathing soft and consistent. This may be inhaling for 2 seconds and exhaling for 4 seconds with an inconsequential pause as air enters and leaves the lungs. We use the out-breath to relax the body and discover a movement pathway that uses the least effort. The most direct route to standing may not be the most efficient. It is through breath and relaxation that we discover how our body would like to move rather than the goal-directed movement commanded by the mind. By letting go of the goal and trusting in the process, we come to enjoy discovering new movement pathways. We find that learning new movement becomes free of time and agenda. In this manner body intelligence is naturally assimilated, similar to what occurs in play.

We can deepen body intelligence further still, through fear inoculation. When we face fear through breath and relaxation, we discover our instincts. The body can move instinctually, much faster than our conscious processing. It is only after the movement has been performed that we realise our actions. Because these movements are instinctual, they are free of technique. These movements cannot be taught, but they can be evoked through fear. For example, we can play a game where we are required to spin until we suddenly decided to fall to the ground. It is impossible for us to find the most efficient pathway for falling because of the innumerable positions from which we can fall. We instead focus on breath and relaxation. Each time we intentionally fall to the ground, we discover that we have no choice but to rely on our breath because when the mind gets in the way, we risk injuring ourselves. Using breath and relaxation, we progressively retrain the nervous system so that stress becomes a trigger for relaxation rather than fight or flight. We find fun in what was once fear-inducing. In this manner we learn about our instincts and we come to trust our own body.

Tradition of the Warrior - Story of internal victory

Outcasted. He cannot go back. Forsaken by the very tradition he was born to protect, Razul no longer knows what it means to move forward. Even death cannot save him, for a noble death is what sets a warrior free. Rejected by the gates of hell, his is an existence in suspense. A ghost of the shadows, he lurks about the forests with humiliation deep in his bones. His heart cold as the ice below his feet; his eyes swollen with a blackness that the devil himself envies.

It was 1684 when Razul - a noble warrior on the outskirts of the Novosibirsk region in Siberia, was captured, tortured and starved by malicious bandits who terrorized his village. He was kept in a cell not high enough to sit nor long enough to lie. Razul, a man broken in body and in mind.

It was a moonless night eight years later, when the power of the aging rebel leader was tested by a ferocious young monster called Graska. The turmoil gave Razul the slightest opportunity to strangle the gatekeeper as he was distracted by the vicious scene. Razul's escape went unnoticed as Graska who stood 2.3 meters tall with deceptive strength and agility had overturned the leadership of the malicious maniacs. With Graska at the helm, the bandits suddenly gained even darker intentions.

Razul disappears into the forest, his tracks easily traceable in the snow yet the bandits had lost interest in him as their new leader fascinated their insanity. Razul's crumbled body lumbers through the forest like a half eaten animal. In the silence of the night, he arrives at the house he once remembered as his own. After repeated knocking, the door finally opens. A man stands in front of him with anger welling up in him at the sight of the disfigured Razul. 'Make him go away' says Razul's wife from a distance. The man at the door steps forward to push Razul away. But Razul had seen enough. He grabs the man by the neck and starts to strangle him. The man is strong. He easily overpowers Razul and starts to menacingly kick his broken body to the ground. As Razul's wife breaks the scene, she recognizes her previous husband, but instantly pretends that she does not know him. Razul is dragged out of the house his father had built and dumped on the streets.

Razul, a warrior of a noble tradition had assaulted a man who had done him no harm. His emotions had overpowered him. The tradition that ran strong in his blood was as distant to him as his once elite body. Blood and bone exposed to the snow, his crippled body crawls back into the depths of the forest. Decimated by the cold, he creeps into a vacant bear's den. Despite the risk of the bear returning, Razul finally relaxes in the comfort of resting his body unconfined for the first time in eight years.

It is the chattering of the birds that wakes him up the next morning. He crawls out of the den like a corpse irritated from being unearthed. He scavenges for edible roots and grubs and satisfied that he has enough energy for the day, he builds himself a rudimentary shelter. Before night fall, he sets up snares to trap small mammals. In the days that follow, Razul starts to mend his disfigured body. He uses a sling that he weaved from dried vines to force his body back into place. He lifts rocks to restore strength in his joints. As his posture improves, he realises that his lower back is hunched. Razul is unable to stand up straight, nor can he bend forward. He can barely reach his knees with his fingers. To do so causes him severe pain. As the months pass by, Razul comes to live with pain.

Still, he continues to mend his body. His bones become unbreakable. His strength and agility go beyond his former glory. His senses heighten as he becomes acquainted with the unforgiving nature. Yet his mind remains broken. The taste of death on his lips, his heart as dark as his eyes. The pain in his back accompanying him in his daily movement.

One day Razul captures a tanuki[10] that puts up a fierce battle. The creature seems to come back to life no matter how powerful the blow to its head. Eventually, Razul outlasts the battle and the meal replenishes the energy he had spent scrambling with the creature. Satisfied by the first meat he has eaten in years, he gets inspired to weave the tanuki hide into a hat. Absorbed in crafting his headpiece, he does not notice a ravenous bear approaching the smell of blood. Suddenly, there is commotion. The bear roars in agony as Razul shivers from the immensity of its ferocity. The bear, disturbed by being hit by an invisible force reluctantly turns away from Razul and disappears into the woods.

In the bear's place stand two hooded figures. A slender old man and a young boy who is rather obese. Razul thanks them for saving his life. The old man sees the suffering written in Razul's body. He asks Razul to stand up straight. Razul does as asked and roars with pain by doing so. The old man asks Razul to relax his body if he wishes to stand in his strength. Razul protests saying that he is strong despite his back pain. The old man looks to the young boy and motions to him to lie flat on his back. The young boy does so without a word. The old man than looks to Razul and asks him lie next to the boy and then roll over him. Razul thinks that this is some form of joke and drops to the ground in an attempt to show his skill. Razul attempts to roll over the boy. To his dismay, the boy moves at a speed that Razul is unable to comprehend. This obese boy moves like an octopus in the water. It is as if the boy is somehow able to shape shift. Unable to roll over this formless giant, Razul finds himself repeatedly humiliated and eventually admits defeat.

'You must forget movement and simply focus on breath to relax,' says

10 Tanuki is a raccoon-like creature from Siberia.

the old man. With these words, they leave Razul.

Once a noble warrior, Razul refuses to believe that it is breath that would grant him victory. Still, he knows that the mysterious figures were once Cossacks who have gone rogue. Cossacks were mythical in their abilities and it was true that Razul was defeated by an obese boy. So Razul takes a deep breath in. He feels the air fill his lungs. He deflates his body with a long exhalation. In one breath, he realises that his entire body is in a state of shock. The tension in his lower back violently holds on to the rest of his structure to give him his distorted shape. Razul begins to breathe deeply and his body begins to feel heavy with exhaustion. His head droops forward and he begins to relax to the pull of gravity. He bends to the point where his fingers reach for his knees. His breath relaxes the tension held by his nervous system. Slowly, he feels his muscles unlocking and his structure reshaping to help him descend even further. His body self-adjusts while Razul loosens himself with each prolonged exhalation. Without any pain, his hands finally reach the ground. His nervous system is not done yet, his hips continue to rotate and deeply open his structure. Razul has now bent to the point where his head is touching his knees. This is further than he has ever been, even before his back pain. He uses his breath to gently stand up and feels that the pain is still there but to a lesser degree.

Razul sits on the ground and tries to straighten his legs. His back pain prevents him from doing so. He again surrenders to breath. He finds that the tension in his hips begins to release. As his legs slowly straighten, he finds that his right leg is having more trouble relaxing to the ground than his left. As Razul breathes deeply, the tension on the outside of his right thigh begins to form into a lump the size of his fist. The lump of energy begins to travel towards his hips as his muscles loosen their grip on his right leg. The lump reaches his right glute where it causes severe pain. Razul continues to relax his nervous system; breath is his only hope. The lump of energy travels further up his body as the acute tension in his hip is released. The lump suddenly propels into his stomach where it begins to untwist like two tangled ropes being separated from each other. Razul does not feel pain, but instead an enormous amount of grief. He begins to moan for no reason. His moan turns into a sob, overwhelmed by sensations that are not in his control.

Razul collapses on the ground. Unable to interfere with the processes occurring in his body, he once more finds comfort in breath. He finds his body searching for movement. With breath as his only guide, a certain relaxation takes over his movement. His spine becomes tension-less as he moves. He does not understand how his body is producing such a continuous flow of movement yet it gives him a sense of freedom that he never knew before. As he rolls, twists and turns on the ground, his mind begins to be released from the trauma held by the body. He finds himself withdrawing into a foetal position as his body unlocks various pathways. After what seems like days of pleasure from the release of pain, he feels the entities of his past loosening their grip on his body.

He stays in a foetal position cocooned by the earth around him; his body experiences a sensation of inhabiting itself for the first time. Razul begins to feel an ever-growing pleasure from feeling his own body. His body finally releases itself from the cage of the mind, speaking a voice that Razul had forgotten. His body had stopped 'speaking' when Razul had withdrawn from the fascination of his innate movements to one that was purely command-based. Such movements had come from self-absorbed thoughts and such thoughts had propelled him into disembodiment. His command-based warrior mentality had educated him out of his body. He had forgotten what it felt like to splash his feet in a puddle of water. He feels a sort of nostalgia for something he did not know he craved for, and a surge of apology to his body for always operating from the needs of the mind. For the disapproval of play. For having regarded the limitations of his body as an inconvenience in the path of a warrior. He kisses his left shoulder in appreciation and for the first time experiences self-love. A surge of emotion erupts from his heart. All his senses merge into an ecstatic harmony. He falls in love with his body, unable to see imperfection. He falls in love with it, not because of the aesthetics that define the proportions of beauty but because it is his! His body is the source of love; it brings a youthful smile to his face, purifies his mind and brings it into a state of clarity, one that exists because his body feels safe. He realises that it is his breath that relaxes his body into a state of security, free of shame and guilt. He feels the love that comes from the depth inside.

Razul surfaces from the womb of the earth with unending strength. The eternal strength of love. The tension in his back came from the entity of insecurity in his own body. The entity that blocked his true strength, now an illusion of the past. Nature had reminded him of his own nature. It is then that Razul decides to return once again to the village he was born to protect. He sets on foot for two days before arriving in a desolate land. He walks towards his house, now a pile of rubble, knowing all too well that he is surrounded by the ghosts of Graska.

Without warning his body sways out of the way and a knife pierces his clothing. He is suddenly circled by fourteen formidable bandits. Each one armed with ruthless insanity. Razul stands tall in his strength, unthreatened. The bandits attack before he has a chance to speak. Knifes and fists come from all directions. Razul's breath flows effortlessly, redirecting the sensations he feels on his body. The skills Razul learnt as a warrior are put in service to the intelligence of the body. The bandits strike each other yet are unable to touch him. Defeated by a man who showed no aggression towards them, the bandit leader Graska appears from the shadows. Towering over Razul he attempts to grab the figure in front of him. Razul simply relaxes out of his reach. Graska's body begins to shudder with an anger that shakes the ground. Graska starts to move at a speed that Razul cannot see. Razul however, has surrendered to his instincts. His body relaxes each time he gets hit. The mighty Graska feels like he is hitting a cloud of smoke. No matter how hard he hits, Razul's body remains unharmed. Graska eventually weakens. Razul simply walks away from him with neither pleasure nor guilt. Enraged, Graska uses his last ounce of energy to spear his body into the formless Razul, only to propel head first into a pile of rubble. With the fearsome Graska killed by his own strength, the malicious bandits disappear into the shadows once more. Razul returns back to his house. He begins to place one stone at a time to rebuild the house as his father once did. Outcasted, yes. He is a warrior free from tradition.

★ ★ ★

Breath and relaxation dissolve the separation between mind and body. Embodiment gives us trust in our instincts. Instincts propel us into a perpetual state of flow and flow gives pleasure to our own movements. Finally, pleasure kindles childlike play, the eternal fountain of youthfulness. The more we dedicate ourselves to nurturing the body, the more we deepen in self-love, the love that radiates through our hearts. It is through self-love that we honour the body. Through self-love we remember the intelligence that pervades the chaos of the mind. It is through self-love that we learn to inhabit our own body.

Intelligence of the Moment

Wisdom consists of unnecessary
accumulation of ideas
put together by people
wishing to define
standards of behaviour
instead of respecting
the mysteries of life

~ Paulo Coelho

Perhaps it is not creativity that is elusive, but that which makes this moment unforgettable.

Our denial of the present moment keeps us trapped in the illusion of destination. We consume each moment by doing things, thinking about our hopes and aspirations for the future. We consume the moment with the illusion of getting somewhere with our lives, with a self-enhanced autobiography of achievements, with the subjective importance we place on ourselves. This is precisely why we suffer. We suffer because we distract ourselves from the inevitability of this moment. The terrible truth is that there is no meaning in what we do. No matter what we do, it is never enough. This is the illusion that traps us in the repetitive cycle of seeking the next possibility for fulfilment. The endpoint we struggle to reach is the very goal that deprives us of fulfilment. The goal is nevertheless justified by our love for the process. This is the unspoken beauty contained within the terrible truth. There is no meaning in what we do, but rather joy pours into what we do. It is then that we realise that it doesn't matter what we do; we find profound satisfaction from deep within.

Why then do we evade this precious moment? Where is the lighter when the candle is lit? We do not hold on to concepts once the idea is grasped. Far too often we forget the lesson and keep the experience. We want to share what we know. This is not wisdom, it is knowledge that is explicit. This knowledge, that we remind ourselves of, is trapped in time. We delve in opinions, predictions and strategies for the way forward. It is through the past that we anticipate the future. Living this moment as if it were yesterday.

The explicit exists because the evolution of the brain has been shaped by fear. Fear signifies importance. If a memory triggers fear, it becomes important. If an emotion triggers fear, it becomes important. If our sensors perceive fear, it becomes important. The brain network that induces fear becomes dominant and begins to work in isolation. The lack of integration in our brain means that networks such as emotion and rationality no longer work in collaboration. The isolated processing gives rise to the explicit form of thinking: linear, unidirectional and goal-directed. And because neurons that fire together, wire together, this basic biological process gets reinforced. Explicit[11] thinking anticipates a number of different possibilities and then decides on the most likely outcome. This type of thinking becomes very efficient because it knows a strategy has predictable results. The simulation of possibilities means that explicit thinking has a high cognitive load and because neurons fire together, wire together, the explicit reinforces the patterns that we see in our lives. The lack of cognitive flexibility means that thinking explicitly works poorly under uncertainty. This is the great paradox: uncertainty induces fear and gives rise to explicit thinking, precisely the type of thinking that works poorly under uncertainty. And because we know no other way, we stick to patterns we have known all our lives. In this manner, fear begins to shape our nervous system and unfortunately, explicit thinking becomes the dominant form of thinking in our society. So we live life in a hurry and the sympathetic fear responses becomes our baseline.

The *explicit* exists as long as the mind is eluded by time. It is the trap of time that gives rise to our strategies. The strategies that govern us are those we gain from times of difficulty, the times when we faced tragedy, the times we overcame misery. However, instead of learning the lesson and letting go of the experience, we choose to keep the strategies even when they are no longer needed. The recycling of our experiences triggers a strategy. These may not be the best, but are protective mechanisms that sometimes overstay their welcome. We quickly forget

11 This is the Bayesian probabilistic approach that has lead to the computational understanding of the brain.

the lesson and return to our safety net, our strategy for life.

Why focus on a strategy when we have no power over the outcome?

Knowledge is irrelevant without un-learning. Like breaking a bad habit, we un-learn knowledge in order to transform it into intelligence.

Rare is the parasympathetic[12] state when our nervous system is calm and relaxed. The state that gives rise to the intelligence of the moment: the *implicit* intelligence. Lacking an overall strategy or plan, the implicit is responsive to the moment. Free from time, the implicit does not incur the high cognitive load that comes from chronic thinking. We may think the implicit is impulsive and unsure, however, it is quite the contrary. This is the other great paradox: the implicit gives us the most certainty. The implicit has no interest in the outcome, so we feel safe to explore all possibilities. With the nervous system in a parasympathetic state we find harmony in the networks of our brain and body. We find congruence between our brain networks rather than a conflict between emotion and rationality. Knowledge that is unlearned self-assembles in response to the present moment. The implicit integrates everything we have learnt to respond to what is happening right now. This is the embodiment of truth. This is the only time when we have a genuine response to the moment. Yet because the sympathetic state (explicit) has become the predominate state of our societies, we have lost touch with the implicit, almost entirely.

Implicit intelligence is acquired in one of three ways:

Errorless – Learning is so inconsequential that the learner is unaware that any learning is taking place. This is the chef who combines ingredients intuitively. When asked of the recipe, he does not know what he did. He simply did what he felt in the moment. This is the musician who forgets that he is playing in front of an audience. The song takes a shape of its own and the music becomes a journey to an unimagined landscape. When asked of the song, the musician is unaware of what he had played. Then

12 The parasympathetic state is when the nervous system is under rest and restoration pro-cesses for homeostasis.

one day, the chef simply picks his favourite recipes and effortlessly puts together a recipe book. The musician begins to talk of acoustic thinking. He is able to describe his music as an architect would describe design. Errorless learning is akin to play. Children learn miraculously because they are yet to understand the concept of failure. Perhaps this is why it is through play that evolution has decided to learn.

Analogy – Learning through an unrelated activity and is sometimes referred to as skill transfer. This is the young man who is enchanted by Cuban salsa. He joins the dance class and becomes suddenly aware of the stiffness in his body, the hesitation in his movement and the lack of firmness in his stance. As he progresses in the dance classes, he realises he is softer in his group conversations, decisive in his thinking and exuberant in his presence. Our propensities are replicated in all aspects of our lives. By facing one of our fears, we face them all.

Cognitive Stacking – Learning a primary task by paying attention to a secondary task. This is the mother who pays deliberate attention to her own presence as her autistic child goes through cycles of sudden outbursts. It is not her insistence to cease the tantrum but the tenderness in her voice that calms her son. It is our inner state that determines the quality of our outcome.

Implicit intelligence is cognitively stable because it is independent of context (Analogy) robust to stress (Cognitive Stacking) and inherently enjoyable (Errorless Learning). Because we deny the inevitability of this moment, we have forgotten this internal alignment that is congruent with all else.

Accessing Intelligence

Why is it that ideas become elusive when we think explicitly yet arise out of 'nowhere' when we are taking a quiet walk through our favourite park or are in the shower?

The mind is able to time-travel. We can travel back in time to moments that we hold dear. We can project forward in time and see our dreams come to life. This ecosystem of realities coexist in our minds, displacing us from the present moment. The mental time anomaly means that the body is fighting against this moment; the indivisible body cannot be in two places at once. When the mind is chronically displaced back in time we face depression and when we are chronically looking into the future, we face anxiety. To prevent our intelligence from being hijacked by time, we guide the attention of the mind into the body. The body is our anchor[13] in the present. We use our breath to establish the connection between brain and body, to release our nervous system from time-driven dissonance.

When the nervous system is relaxed, we are able to access implicit intelligence in real-time. It is our devotion to this moment that frees us. This is the paradox, it is discipline that gives us freedom. We do not need to wait any longer to be free of time. By unlearning our explicit knowledge, we disassemble what we know. How intelligence is reassembled is entirely dependent on the moment. We no longer segment reality into measurable units to avoid comprehending what we cannot understand. When linearised thought patterns are liberated from our self-referential timeline, our intelligence gains an intuitive ability that is aligned with the incomprehensible. We begin to draw from the multidimensional possibilities that are only available to us in this moment.

This is the traveller who sets off on a journey without a plan because in every journey there is a hidden story that no amount of planning can reproduce. This is the traveller who speaks to the one stranger amongst many, an hour before he is about to board his flight to Geneva. It is the stranger's last few words that set in motion the changes that happen in the traveller's life for the next five years.

We know very little about the reasons why some of our life-changing decisions are made abruptly. Perhaps the forces that evoke these decisions

13 Brain-body congruence is known as vagal tone. The higher the vagal tone, the better the communication between brain and body.

are not at all foreign but simply overwritten from the lack of sensitivity to our own body. The visceral compass is embedded in the intelligence of the body. In every moment we experience an autonomic[14] response. For simplicity, we shall isolate these sensations to the heart. The heart is sensitive to each moment[15] and is the first reference point to our perception of reality. The cardiac pulmonary response shapes all the process upstream that eventually shapes our thoughts and behaviours[16]. With the mind silent, we can listen to the voice of the heart. We commit to the heart without question because love was never meant to be understood.

We may walk past the same stranger each day without questioning where he is going. Then one day the stranger feels the love that radiates from our heart. He impulsively invites us to the jazz night he plays at. There we meet the woman of our wildest dreams because she too was invited by someone she had just met on the subway back home. It is by opening our hearts that we find each other.

The father is worried by the company his son keeps. He wants to intervene, to guide his son into morality and the greater good. His mind confirms that this is what is best for his son. His heart says 'love your son without reason'. The father listens to his heart. The son learns lessons of betrayal and deceit by his friends and discovers self-respect. He honours his father for being there for him when times were hard. He matures into morality on his own terms. His morality matches the circumstances that influence his life.

The young woman never knows which path to take. There are too many possibilities. She is good at communication, problem solving and learning new skills. Everyone loves her company and her managers recommend her highly. Yet she never sticks to anything she is good at. She thinks that

14 Autonomic refers to all the process that occur by itself such as digestion, breathing, immune function and is regulated by the vagus nerve.

15 Our breath is the bridge between the external and the internal. Our breath changes with the moment. The breath is intrinsically linked with the heart and is what gives rise to heart rate variability (HRV). Therefore the heart is inevitably sensitive to this moment.

16 See Smith et. al. (2017) *The hierarchical basis of neurovisceral integration*

she must make all the wrong decisions before she makes the right one. Yet not once has she considered what she wants. She has always done what appears pleasing in the eyes of others and in doing so, allowed society to transform her into something she is not. She will not allow herself the one possibility that will dissolve all of her confusion: to think for herself. One day there will be a job that is perfect for her. It is much safer this way than considering the yearnings of her own heart. This is what she thinks.

No 'body' can be in two places at once[17]. Our visceral intelligence is therefore true to the moment. Each time we are greeted by choice, we feel it in our hearts. If there is ambiguity, we imagine each possibility without any attachment to the outcome. We consider the first possibility. We imagine it in evocative detail and then let go of the possibility completely. We then consider the second possibility with just as much conviction and without any interest in the outcome. The heart will find one possibility more expansive than the other. We go along with the possibility that delights the heart. We do so without reason or question. This is the intelligence that we access in this moment. This is the intelligence that we cannot comprehend yet we never regret when we look back.

The Forbidden Intelligence - Story of possibility

It was three years ago that April was in Bali on a two week holiday. She went on the tourist trails, visited ancient temples, went to the monkey forest, climbed the volcano at sunrise and enjoyed the raw vegan delicacies in Ubud. She then returned back to her life as an architect on 5th Avenue, Seattle. April was in her late twenties. She had a fabulous apartment and close friends that she felt were her surrogate family. She loved her job in a city that was large enough to promise the opportunities that exist in the high-rises yet small enough to move at a friendly pace.

A month after her return from Bali, April met Pau, a Spanish man

17 We cannot be in two places at once, at least not until we are freed from time. See next chapter - Flow in Synchronicity.

from Barcelona. Pau was in his late forties. A wild businessman who had earned his money in real-estate, he now lived in secret locations around the world—places where the rich find their uninterrupted paradise. This was the type of paradise where young models get special passes to secluded islands only accessible by boat. The paradise is heightened at night through LSD and trance music because on an island where there is nothing to do, we get bored very quickly.

April has ravenous pleasure with Pau. He is extremely audacious in romance. He has a chic social profile and he is oblivious to rules and regulations. Money is his currency for freedom. Pau visits April a few times a month. Although April knows that Pau is with other women when he is visiting his paradises, she never brings up the subject. Her jealousy makes Pau even more desirable to her. She also knows that, even though Pau pays for their nights out and buys her lingerie, their relationship, if there is one, will be short-lived.

On a Wednesday morning, she is having a meeting with a client on 5th Avenue when her mind suddenly feels distracted with thoughts of Pau. The meeting becomes a blur and she walks out of it with no idea what was discussed. She immediately gets on the phone to Pau who does not answer. In her anxiety, April tries to contact him several times during the day and eventually gets a message that he has got a gorgeous new apartment with the largest balcony in Dubai. He offers to fly her over for the experience. April kindly declines his offer and their lack of contact over the next days becomes an unspoken understanding that it is now all over between them.

The dreamlike reality that Pau had created dries up into the everyday reality of a life that was once meaningful to April. Her work becomes devoid of meaning, her friends feel boring and she does not know how to recreate the excitement she felt with Pau. Each day April turns up to work, she loses a part of her soul. She feels trapped inside the walls of an office. All she wants is an escape route out of her life. She works like this for six more months before seeking help. The psychiatrist diagnoses her as clinically depressed and administers 50mg of Zoloft[18] to be taken twice a day.

April arrives at home that evening. As she sits on her bed, her eyes water with tears at the sight of the pills in her hand. She walks over to the bathroom and empties the container of pills, flushing them out of existence. She than checks her emails and ends up mindlessly booking a flight back to Bali. The next morning she checks her emails at work and receives the confirmation of her itinerary to Bali. She suddenly panics realising that her flight is that afternoon. What was she thinking? She calls the airline to cancel her flight. While on the waiting line, the weight of the walls around her begin to squeeze life out of her soul. She slams down the phone and walks into the director's office to announce her resignation. The director listens to her story about depression without interest and then tells her that everyone in the office had seen this coming and were waiting for her to quit. He hands April her redundancy package and wishes her safe travels. April is confused with the ease at which she quit her job, but the thrill of adventure suddenly carries her mind away. Her heart racing, she arrives home. She does not need much more than a few bikinis and a couple of sarongs. Her suitcase packed, she arrives at the airport just two hours after quitting her job.

Bali has changed since she was last there. Or maybe, she has changed? She arrives in the middle of the night. Her suitcase is grabbed by a young Balinese boy the moment she reaches for it from the luggage conveyer belt and the boy immediately darts towards a taxi. April chases the boy pleading for him to stop. With her bag inside the taxi, April is obliged to get in and she is frantically taken to a bungalow. It is not the one she booked but she is too tired to argue with the greedy taxi driver. The bungalow is smaller than she hoped but has a low ceiling fan which soothes her to sleep. The next morning she walks out into the reckless buzz of the streets of Kuta. She feels overwhelmed and confused by why she is in Bali. She had not planned her trip this time and didn't feel like

18 Zoloft is a selective serotonin reuptake inhibitor (SSRI) antidepressant

doing the usual tourist trails. She finds herself in a restaurant with modern food. She is not hungry but orders randomly from the menu. The ocean side cafe brings a warm breeze that wraps like a blanket around her skin. She feels this breeze as if for the first time. The Mediterranean music blends in with the conversations that she hears around her. Her mind drifts into a dreamlike state. Her mind wanders to the islands beyond Bali. It had not occurred to her that there were other islands under the sky. She half finishes her meal and then wanders into a travel booth on the opposite side of the road. She scans the destinations on the map of Indonesia. For reasons not yet apparent to her, she follows her impulse to island-hop east.

Quickly getting bored with each island she arrives at, she finds herself constantly on the move. Eventually she arrives at Flores Island from which she convinces a local fisherman to take her to Komodo Island. The Komodo islands are isolated by strong currents and most fishermen are reluctant to venture into turbulent waters. Alone on a boat with two fishermen she suddenly feels insecure. Drifting in the endless oceanic landscape she scans the horizon for landmarks. As nightfall approaches and the stars descend over the ocean their boat is suddenly surrounded by smaller pirates canoes. The pirates swarm around April demanding her valuables. The local fishermen see the terror in April's eyes and indicate to her to unlock her bags. The pirates raid her bags for money and vanish off the boat just as quickly as they had arrived. Rain beings to fall and the fishermen pull down the covers to keep the rear part of the boat dry. April has a foggy sleep and wakes up the next morning drenched and cold.

The fishermen now see April with different eyes. Last night, they too were terrified by the pirates just as she was. They see before them a woman who is no longer a western cash machine but a human with the same doubts and fears that they have. One of the fishermen takes off the wet sarong from April and wraps her in one of his own dry shirts. It is the first time that April has experienced any comfort from the locals who, until that point, were only after her money. April arrives on Komodo Island and is humbled by the giant dragons who are custodians of this ancient land. The land that confuses her senses; the air is humid, yet the land is dry and arid. The forest is just as ancient as the dragons, and April is teleported back in time. She feels an energy from the land that she does not yet understand. It is as though the land wishes to speak with her. As she walks alone on this barren country with a lush ecosystem one of the dragons rises up on its hind feet. The dragon was invisible to April until it stood up and now she is dangerously close to this ancient monster which is as tall as her. Paralysed by fear, April stares into the eyes of the monster. The ancient eyes explain nothing of themselves. Unthreatened, the monster returns to the ground and approaches April without intention. Shivering with panic, April instinctively makes herself smaller and sits in a squat.

The dragon is now at eye level and only two feet away. April can smell the rotting meat still stuck in the monster's teeth. The dragon turns its head so that one of its eyes stares directly into hers. April and the dragon stare into each other's eyes. The dragon is no longer a monster; April, no longer human. They are both creations of the Great Mother. It is Mother Nature that wishes to see herself; to recognise the delicate life that pre-exists all organisation and hierarchy. The Great Mother who holds us all without fear that she may one day get hurt and does not take sides. The Great Mother who does not say 'this is yours' and 'that is mine'. We cannot own our mother; it is us who belong to the land. The Great Mother knows no separation because no matter what we do with our lives, one day we all return back into her arms to continue the cycle of nature. A tear appears in the eyes of the dragon. April feels an ancient chill that makes her body shiver. The dragon then departs, casually camouflaging back into the landscape.

Aprils walks back to the beach with grief in her heart. She grieves the connection that she did not know she could have with the land. She grieves the distance between her and the Great Mother. She grieves that it did not cross her mind to one day return home. She grieves the tear that reminded her that Mother Nature is not a monster. The fishermen welcome her onto the boat and she solemnly returns back to Flores. The next morning April impulsively books a flight to Jayapura, Irian Jaya.

The lowlands of Jayapura are like floodplains where houses are built on stilts. The ocean feels excessively exposed and April has an unquestionable urgency to visit the highlands. To return to the forest. She makes her way to a nearby military base where she boards a small aircraft with no doors. She sits alongside twenty fully armed soldiers. The aircraft flies over the majestic mountains that would normally be snow-capped, but are instead populated by dense forests since they lie on the equator. These forests are beyond the reach of logging companies since it is absurd to build roads on such slippery slopes. April finds it bewildering witnessing such lush, green jungles in the sky, a domain that would normally be reserved to the clouds alone. The aircraft lands in a valley enveloped by the towering mountains. The soldiers irritatedly throw her backpack out of the aircraft that has no doors. April is then told to find a stranger who speaks the western language in the local bar. She enters the village with several decaying wooden huts and heads towards the only structure that looks like a bar. There she finds the stranger she is looking for. A native man in his mid 50s who speaks a language they both understand.

She learns that the stranger has spent his entire life earning himself five pigs. The western concept of money has little value in the highlands. Five pigs meant that he had earned his tribe's approval to marry. His wife later died. He was once more a man without pigs and without a wife. The stranger escorts April to the only civilized structure in the region, built by missionaries in the 1800s. The château, fortified within a high wall, has an eerie feel, so creepy that April can taste evil in the air. April senses that her room has experienced many deaths and violent acts. The eerie terror keeps her up all night. The next morning the stranger who speaks the language they both understand turns into a native bushman navigating their trek into the mountains, through hidden dwellings, underground caves networks, ancient burial sites and terrifying suspended bridges that feel like they would snap with each step.

At a time when April's heart is agitated with the tension of love, she feels better being constantly on the move in a land that reveals so little of its secrets. The jungle encourages the pursuit of the unknown, a desperate search for the meaning of it all. What are we looking for? Why does the language of the heart elude reason? Her journey in the remote depths of this primeval land becomes a search into the inner depths of her own heart. The inner terrain is troubled, dark and murky, but she knows that this is only the surface. She has to explore deeper.

That night the stranger makes a fire to keep them warm in the hostile night where the air tastes of evil. April cuddles into the arms of the stranger. Feeling protected by someone more powerful than she is, she falls into a trance-like sleep. The whispers of Mother Nature lures her deeper into her inner exploration. Beyond the body, beyond what we know as physical. There is no darkness; there is no light, only an endless void. A void without dimension, a void undefined by time. Unable to comprehend, her mind abandons this inner journey. A new awareness awakens in her and displaces her departing mind. She finds herself moving faster than the speed of light, yet simultaneously remaining in one place. She experiences the tiniest electrons rotating around atoms to galaxies colliding against each other all at once. She experiences the entire history of the earth from the evolution of dinosaurs to the extinction of man in an instant. Her mind momentarily appears within the undescribed. But the answers come before any question arises; her initial questions fail to register. What to do with her career? What to do with relationships? How will she die? All are answered simultaneously.

It is the sound of the birds that wake her up in the morning. She feels disoriented since in the formless dimension she did not have direction. The pain of the earth suddenly fills her heart. She feels terribly guilty for being human. She feels responsible for inflicting the history of crimes on earth and on people. Yet before the mind enters a thought spiral, she is drawn once again into her inner state. All that exists becomes equanimous again. In the presence of the inner dimension, all doubts of the mind disappear. She no longer seeks answers. She realises that there is no going back. She had been navigating her life in the dark and the light in her heart had just been switch on. She lets go of her trust in the unknown because there is nothing to be convinced of anymore. Doubt and fear were simply products of the mind. Now that she has had a taste of a deeper dimension, the mind understands its unimportance. Her mind simply steps aside in reverence of a higher intelligence.

April thanks the mysterious forces that removed all obstacles from her path, the moment she stepped towards herself. She opens her eyes once more for the first time. The stranger is sitting in front of her. April sees the face of the Great Ape before her. The face that on the surface has colour but beneath the skin is moved by blood and bone that is the same in all. His face bares the history of his people and the union of his mother and his father. It shares with the world his every emotion and contorts with the darkness of despair. It has been carved by tears because he has been broken time and time again. Yet, he is unable to hold back a smile when he unearths the root crops he has planted many moons ago. The expression on his face is a creation of this moment. The stranger sees in April's face that which remains unspoken. They walk down the forest trail and cross a suspended bridge that leads to a cluster of huts. The women in the village are cooking a meal under the earth. After the meal of roots that April does not know the name of, the kids follow her everywhere she goes. Their eyes have not witnessed what lies beyond the mountains. They breathe the air that tastes of evil. Yet the kids smile because they know nothing of money. The internet does not exist. Tonight the men will come back from the forest with a beast that will feed their village. A man with twenty pigs will have four wives. It rained two weeks ago and there is enough water in the well. The kids smile because they do not yet have a reason not to. April loses interest in the pace she was travelling at. To constantly bolt from one destination to another. She sits with the women who weave baskets from dried vines, her mind no longer running to places distant to this moment. She simply observes the tedious process with fascination. The stranger interrupts the women and informs April that the next military aircraft will leave the next morning.

It takes four days for April to arrive back to Seattle. The trip back is uneventful as itineraries go, but within April everything has changed. She does not once rush to her connecting flight. She looks deeply into the eyes of each person who sits next to her. There is little need for words. Upon arriving in Seattle, the thought of finding a job crosses her mind, which immediately feels too limited an archetype to work within. Looking out of her apartment window, she calls Pau. In the fragrant forests of Costa Rica, Pau answers her call with mild surprise. April speaks of her intuition to visit him to which Pau fiercely agrees. She sells all her belongings and terminates her apartment lease. With the lightness of leaving everything behind she arrives to a treetop villa in Costa Rica. Her heart is warmed by the sunlight filtering through her luscious canopy nest. She takes a week to simply be held in the arms of the earth. One evening Pau treats her to a decadent dinner of well-aged moussaka and champagne. April's heart radiates with the love of being treated like a queen. That night she wears an auburn-pink dress and her hair glistens like the gentle ocean at sunset. She gets up to dance, and is engulfed by the romance of Latin music. She is suddenly taken by strong arms that glide her off the floor. A young man with mysterious blue eyes and a broad chest melts her into seduction. Their bodies tantalised by sensual bliss. Without words, they give themselves to each other. They return to the treetop villa. That night April sleeps in the arms of this mysterious man. The next morning, the man makes breakfast with some porridge mixed with local spices and sticks of cinnamon. He also makes some tea out of reishi mushrooms. April comes to learn that this man is an expert in bushcraft and medicinal plants. Curious about the secrets that Mother Nature reveals so little of, April decides to learn from this man for as long as it feels right.

Five years on, April travels the world running nature retreats on interspecies communication. She communicates the subtle messages to heal the relationship between men and the natural world. She trains seasoned veterinarians on how to work with animals. She gets featured in documentaries and news networks around the world. Her work makes a strong impression on governments and other policy makers to protect land that they know little of. Yet she lives a humbling life in the Serengeti National Park, Tanzania, East Africa.

★ ★ ★

When doubt and fear disappear, the doors open into a different state, implacable in its purity. The purity of intelligence is inseparable from our heart's desire and cannot exist outside this moment. With the world no longer in our control, our senses break free and we begin to commune directly with the world. The mysterious connection returned forever to this moment. No longer misled by the temptations of desire, our only hope becomes a certainty. In this moment we forgive the past—that which is no longer relevant. For this moment becomes visible when the past is forgotten. We let go of the future. For the destination is this moment. We open the eyes of our heart. We realise that love is the answer only because we created a question. Love was there from the very start. The love that we pour into what we do is evident in what we create. End and means are one.

Flow State

The wind
can go
and come back
whenever it wants to
it can change direction
without ever
having to explain
why

~ Paulo Coelho

When the Angel of Death comes to greet us, we are willing to change anything, even when it leads to suffering, if we survive that is. There are no discussions.

We are willing to change for death, yet in life we shield ourselves from change. Because planning is helpful. But when change arrives, it asks us to cast aside all that we had prepared for. We find ourselves limited by our comforts and protective beliefs. Suddenly we do not wish to face the unthought-of. So we practice resilience, we struggle against adversity because we believe that by overcoming our obstacles we become stronger. We become defiant in resisting the inevitable. Then the moment arrives when we have spent all the energy that we could squeeze out of ourselves. We become exhausted and lifeless. We lose perspective of what we were so forcefully defending. Lost and confused, we don't know what we want, so we seldom know which direction to take. We complain that life is testing us. Yet when change knocked at our door, we were the ones who challenged the inevitable.

Then life throws in another struggle because lessons do not go away until we have learnt them. And because we have nothing left to spend, we let go of our control. It is in this moment that we realise we are the ones weighing heavily on life. We are the ones manipulating and trying to influence life. Whatever we are trying to control is illusion. Life was never in our control in the first place. There are forces at play that are beyond what we will ever know. No matter how strong our identity, we cannot defeat our fate. We find that the sharpest sword cannot scratch the surface of water. It is then that we become like water; the water that flows down mountains, carving valleys into rivers and yielding flowers wherever it flows. Life-giving water lets everything flourish by itself. Until one day, the river arrives at the ocean: the very origins of life itself.

It is the great act of surrender that prepares us to begin life. We surrender for anything less is an obstacle to flow. It is to life that we surrender. Because we are life. We take a breath into existence and step out of the way for an act, far greater than ourselves, to flow through us. We align with forces yet unknowable. We surrender for we know not what is good nor what is bad. Every misfortune is an opportunity. Surrender is the alchemy that unlocks the possibility in each catastrophe. For we cannot foresee magic. We cannot make magic happen. Through surrender we are liberated from our linear thought patterns. In this moment we can only discover all that is new. For as long as life exists, it will strip us of illusion until each encounter becomes a unique surprise and we become responsive to the mysteries of the unknown.

For some, it is this mystery that excites. This is the adventurer who travels to distant lands to encounter the unfamiliar. This is the thrill seeker who trusts his instincts in the abyss, somewhere between life and death. This is the woman who is addicted to promiscuity because sex is always better the first time. It is these activities that dissolve our self-centric beliefs and fuels us with an energy that is far greater than what we know as our own. We sometimes call this being in 'the zone' or 'flow state'. But when the adventurer returns home, he quickly gets bored. It is routine that scares him. He reluctantly finds a job only to save up for his next adventure. The thrill seeker bears the scars of close encounters with death. Yet death no longer scares him so he takes bigger and bigger risks. The woman falls in love but struggles with the patterns that she has learnt from being promiscuous.

To be sure, flow does not come from what we do, it is a state. [19]. Hence, the term 'flow state'.

Flow has 5 core characteristics according to Mihaly Csikszentmihalyi who conceptualised its theory in psychology:

---

19 In psychology a state is different from emotion which has a short latency and mood that lasts longer, perhaps a few hours. Our state is governed by our neurochemical baseline. For example, we can be in a depressive or hedonic state. To shift a state requires us to change our entire neurochemical balance leading to a new disposition.

Effortless – There is no resistance in what we are doing. It happens naturally.

Automatic – There are no thoughts interfering with what we do. We execute through an empty mind.

Peak Creativity – We go beyond our habitual cognitive thresholds.

Intrinsic Motivation – There is so much joy pouring into what we do, that what produces flow is its own reward.

Timelessness – Hours disappear in minutes, yet we do not want the moment to end.

We, as the human species, have the remarkable ability to become self-aware. This has led to enormous acts of self-dominance. The acute concentration of a gymnast to control their body is unparalleled in the animal kingdom. The incredible ability of free-divers to suppress the compulsion to breathe is the extent to which we have dominance over our own mind. To this end Mihaly Csikszentmihalyi states that 'the easiest step towards improving the quality of life consists in simply learning to control the body and its senses.' However, flow was never a lifestyle choice nor an activity. The ultimate act of self-dominance is to let it all go. Surrender is our greatest strength. The limitations of mind and body no longer have any power over us. We let go of the outcome and trust in the process. Our bodies crave flow. The visceral experience of being in perfect harmony with the present moment. The precise communication[20] between brain, body and behaviour creates the perfect relationship within ourselves and therefore with all of existence.

Flow is the very human state that is aligned with the incomprehensible. In this state we become the embodiment of intelligence. It is not the characteristics of flow but its prerequisites that allow us to embody the endless intelligence we call flow. These prerequisites include:

---

20 Each neural network of the brain has small-world properties. Gamma synchrony occurs when neural networks work synergistically, measured through electroencephalography (EEG). This cohesive experience of consciousness is known as neural binding.

Breath - There is no fear. We use breath[21] to relax the nervous system. We feel safe to explore possibility.

Relaxation - There is no doubt. With our brain and body working synergistically, our mental dissonance dissolves leaving behind profound clarity.

Intelligence - There is no linearity. With our undivided attention on this moment, we become aware of the intelligence that is beating in our own heart.

When we apply breath and relaxation to our daily lives, we find that our habitual patterns begin to break down. No amount of programs that work on behaviour change paradigms are able to do this. When stress becomes a trigger for relaxation, we have rewired the survival response to one that is parasympathetic. In doing so, we reprogram our visceral response and shift our entire state of being. By working with our visceral intelligence, we go beyond programs that simply work on the body[22] and those that simply work on the mind[23]. The brain is rooted in the body through the spinal cord. The spinal cord originates from the base of the brain, known as the brainstem. Similar to the stem of a tree, the brainstem is the point from which all other 'branches' of the brain proliferate. The tenth cranial nerve from the brainstem descends deep into the body and is known as the vagus nerve. More than 85 percent of the information travelling in the vagus nerve is travelling upwards, providing the brain[24] with visceral information. However, this information has become unavailable since the evolution of humankind has been hijacked by the increase in brain size. Today we have become so reliant on the brain that we have lost our visceral intelligence. When we are in nature, we experience it with all of our senses. In the world today, we are under the spell of technology, experiencing it compulsively

21 See section of breath in chapter 4 for techniques to relax the nervous system

22 Referring to various forms of bodywork and fitness trends

23 Referring to psychology, psychiatry, personal coaching and the like

24 McCraty 2014 et. al *Cardiac coherence, self-regulation, autonomic stability, and psycho-social well-being*

through our heads. In fact, observe what happens to our posture when we are consumed by technology. We do not experience our handheld devices, viscerally through our body as we do a jacaranda tree in full blossom. It is this visceral intelligence that has been neglected by the education system that teaches our children to become chronic thinkers. This system gives meaning to doing, which, in turn, leads to performance addictions. As long as we invest in doing, we will continue to seek meaning in our lives. The currencies of illusion, which include time and money, will keep us trapped in the itinerary that has been appointed by those before us. Our potential will remain unrealised as long as we use illusion to define who we are. Once we break illusions of the system, we become exuberant with the presence that is free from doing. We experience this moment not simply with the mind, but with our full visceral integration. When we are in this moment with our entire essence, flow emanates from deep within us. We respond to this moment, not simply with the fear-driven, goal-directed, linearity of the mind, but with the full alignment of brain and body. The internal harmony within us is felt viscerally, by those around us. This is the harmony that dissolves all conflicts. Solutions are far simpler than anything we can think. It is then that we dance with possibility. We begin to enjoy the benefits of flow when magic becomes apparent in each moment.

Flow in survival

As long as the laws of nature exist, nothing is immune to survival. When an animal is born, its senses immediately guide it towards food. As the animal discovers the unknown territory, its senses alert it to danger. The animal is unaware that it is not immune to death, but nature takes care of this; the animal has an irresistible instinct to mate. Beneath the skin, an organ system regulates digestion, sexual and cardiovascular arousal. The animal knows nothing of this. It only understands food, sex and danger. For the most part, it is food, sex and danger that take priority of our own instincts.

By our very nature, our mouth waters with the smell of our favourite food. There are moments in our lives when we are irresistibly attracted to the opposite sex. Any sudden sounds heighten our heart rate, if even for a moment. When our survival instinct seeks beyond this moment, we lose the harmony between brain, body and behaviour. The relentless struggle for survival becomes one that is in response to lack. We over-consume food because we fear starvation. This internal *lack* makes us lonely so we seek company in order to feel complete. It drives us to obsessively accumulate finances as a safeguard against danger. Despite how much wealth we accumulate, we still feel fear. Without breath and relaxation, the mind is subconsciously driven by scarcity. Breath and relaxation calm the nervous system into a state of security. It is the sense of expansiveness that comes from safety that allows us to access intelligence. This intelligence may seem to be of no use in the present moment. However, without it we may never discover the secret hands that guide and support us. Without surrender we may never develop the blind trust. Without trust in the incomprehensible we may never know that we are always taken care of. Food, sex and danger may remain as our limiting beliefs, the primal self-limitations that keep us trapped in the mundane human experience.

Take finances for example. When money is a limiting belief, we become protective of money despite how much we have. We begin to restrict our lives to conserve money. True, money does not grow on trees. But we cannot eat money. Nature provides all, even water[25] grows on trees. Even as modern humans, we can survive without money all together by simply trusting intelligence[26] to guide us. Whether we follow our dream or simply work for money, we will be confronted by obstacles. We may find happiness in exchanging money for our time. We may happily sell our time but time is something we cannot buy back. Both time and money are currencies of illusion. Once we break our attachment to money, it is

25 Referring to coconut water.

26 One example of thriving without money is the Pixel Trade Project - *http://thepixeltrade.com*

no longer a limiting belief. Then, there are no bounds to what we can give and receive. We give generously simply because wealth comes to those who have it. We receive abundantly because we honour the exchange for our service. We do so without explanation because ultimately every exchange is an act of love.

Flow in Conversation

So many of our thoughts happen in our heads; only a few are communicated verbally. At times, the overwhelming density of our thoughts can become unbearable noise. This noise is evident in our bodies, when we scratch our heads, when we are distracted and unable to maintain eye contact. Our posture is the product of our physiognomy - our chronic structure based on our temperament. The lack of harmony between brain and body means that there is unclarity in what we say. We respond with mixed emotions. Conversations become entrenched in duality and dogma. Because we are unclear in ourselves, there is no amount of communication that can rectify our assertions. Despite language being a small portion of how we communicate, we still chose to quarrel with words. Our thoughts are multidimensional, communicated both verbally and through body language. Yet, when we speak from fear, our thoughts become linear and goal-directed. The response we get is also linear and goal-directed. It does not matter how elaborate an explanation we come up with, we simply defend illusion. The entities that grip our subconscious speak over the voice of the heart.

Unless we speak from the heart, we will feel threatened by sharing truth. So we live in a world where no one speaks up, because nobody else did. Conversations can only begin when there is nothing to say. In this manner we are free of motive or desire. The conversation is no longer a filler for the lack we experience in ourselves. It does not matter how confident we are in what we say, our words are not accepted if they threaten or challenge identity. Yet when our nervous system is relaxed, we find the great gift of transference. Through our nervous system, we viscerally induce relaxation in others because we cannot be heard in a hurry. Transference allows us to speak our hearts and remain unthreatening. Only when we speak to the heart, do we truly speak. Only when we speak to the heart, are we truly heard, whether the mind agrees or not.

It is when we look into each other's eyes that we find ourselves in another. It is without doubt or fear that we communicate the words of love. We let go of politeness because love is unapologetic. Love is communicated not only through appreciation and gratitude but also through ruthless truth and unrelenting composure. It is when we are left with no words that we truly understand each other. This is when we pick up on the intentions of another. Like children, we laugh because we read each other's minds. When we speak, our ideas are an explosion of breakthroughs, unbounded by the edge of possibility. Because our own nervous system is relaxed, we viscerally receive information that we may have previously been insensitive to. As we speak, we may find those whose words are spoken from entities that have consumed the mind. We do not communicate with these entities. We speak directly to the heart. It is through connecting with the heart that illusion is broken, without threatening identity. It is in these moments that our words acquire a timeless dimension. We go further than we think, because the voice of the heart cannot be thought of. It is as if the words of angels are whispered from our lips. The words arrive the moment they are ready to be heard. The immaculate schedule of magic restored to our every union.

Flow in Movement

Movement is the language that the body understands. As we expand in our intelligence, so too does the intelligence of our movement. The prevalence of the explicit is apparent in our movements. A culture where movement has become goal-oriented towards specialising in skill or aesthetic beauty. When movement becomes linear, automated and repetitive, we lose joy in movement itself. It is our landscape that limits our movements into terrifyingly linear patterns. Our sedentary lifestyle takes us deeper into captivity. Our bodies stopped speaking to us the moment we decided that we knew better and designed our own Nature. Loving ourselves is loving nature, because we are Nature. So when we look around, we see how much we love ourselves.

As we impose explicit instructions on the 'correct' alignment and the 'right' technique, we overwrite the body's innate pathways that evolved over millions of years. The inbuilt intelligence in every human body that has been acquired through evolution is far greater than what is written in science literature. When the body's natural ability to autocorrect its posture becomes dormant, we begin to accumulate injuries and unexplained physical pain.

Similar to unlearning knowledge, we unlearn movement so that it becomes a genuine expression to this moment. We may have accumulated movement from various forms of dance, martial arts, athletics and contests. We decentralise these movements until they become free of identity. The weight of tradition lifted, the discipline and dedication embodied. These disassembled units of movements are then available instinctually through breath and relaxation. Our body's innate intelligence restores joy to our every motion. Play, which is a natural part of our animal lineage, becomes a central feature in our daily movements. Play and fear cannot coexist. This is perhaps why play may be the highest form of intelligence.

We may experience this intelligence momentarily in states induced by fear such as combat or trance-like activities like improvised dance. The embodiment of implicit intelligence allows flow to be available consistently. We no longer rely on activity to produce flow. Our movements become frictionless. We find ease as we roll out of bed, lift a cup of tea or hold the hand of our child as we cross the road. Play becomes intrinsically rewarding, an everlasting joy that does not decay with time.

Ultimately, movement is simply kinetic energy. This energy is inseparable from our terrain and gravity. Regardless of whether we sit still, the earth is always rotating. Energy will always be displaced. Our bodies have adapted to this interconnected relationship over millions of years. The constantly shifting nature of energy demands that our movements join forces with each new equilibrium to become one body of moving energy. Rather than controlling the forces acting upon us, we become aware of our own nature. This is how the body remembers what it is.

Flow in Creativity

We express creativity fearlessly for it is the sinking feeling of routine from which the light of creativity gradually vanishes. Until the spark can no longer light the flame. The explicit repeats our reality until it becomes self-perpetuating. We become more and more self-similar by reinforcing our habits and patterns with each new day that passes us by. No amount of explicit learning will bring forth creativity since the true potential of human beings dwells beyond skill itself!

Breath and relaxation may help to overcome our insecurities and offer courage to explore our vulnerabilities. Yet we let go of these techniques in order to lose our minds. When the discipline and technique is outgrown, the embodiment of the flow state becomes our new baseline. We then enter the realm of the untapped. The trance induced by losing ourselves completely evokes epiphanies, spontaneous talents, unexplained inspiration and visions that we would otherwise dare not consider. We connect with a part of ourselves that is primordial and shameless in its wildness. This is the source of creativity.

Creativity is like the wild horses that have a mind of their own. We do not tame creativity. We simply hold on for dear life as it takes us on a wild ride. We care little about the direction we are going because we have travelled the familiar path countless times. We journey unrestricted in our imagination. We suddenly sing a song even if we have never sung before. The romantic fantasies of our feelings put into words. Some may think us mad. Yet we are pleased that we are mad because our heart's desire is far more interesting than any behaviour we are accustomed to. We become strangers to ourselves, curious about how each one of our thought is made, about the birth place of each memory, the taste of each emotion. We become curious of how each thread of thought is woven into the fabric of perception. We patiently unweave the fabric until all threads are unlinked, unordered and individual. We then lose interest in the threads because it was a senseless activity anyway. By foolishly playing with our thoughts we realise that we are brave. It takes great courage to be lost without reason. We learn that by losing, we discover the victory of defeat. The blessing of defeat comes to those who have fought the battles of the mind in the darkness of the night; those who pursued love when it crossed their path despite being rejected time and time again. It is with creativity that we face the doubt that it may not work out. Because each time we see the sparkle in someone's eyes we remember that we can never fail. Failure comes to those who have never lost, those who have avoided risk in fear of humiliation. The only limits to our potential are those we believe in.

Flow in Sex

We make love shamelessly. Like some of our wild relatives, *Homo sapiens* are wired[27] for an enormous sexual appetite. However, the suppression of our libido has denied men and women their natural arousal. The secrecy of sexual practices means that we are bought up in a culture, which objectifies body types, yet deprives us of sexual release. The damaging history of sexual relations has created protective walls within the hearts of men and women. The sexual energy is as deeply rooted as the primal instincts of seeking food

27 See - *Sex at Dawn*. Book by Cacilda Jethá and Christopher Ryan

and avoiding danger. Until we are free of sexual desire, we will be dangerously possessed by it. To be a slave to our sexual desire is contrary to flow.

The horny human seeks out pleasure. Yet the goal-oriented pleasures are short lived. Men convince women of love to get sex and women give in to sex to get love. Each a means to an end. We have confused sex for love. In fact, most relationships end because of the lack of love that we attempt to fill through sex. Love does not come from sex but flows out from the infinite depths of our own heart. Without loving ourselves, we cannot love another. Much like meditation that quietens the mind, celibacy allows us to transmute our sexual energy. We allow the sexual energy to well up in our hearts. It is the amplification of love that frees us from temptations and desire. We end the affair with infatuation. We let go of the love that is based on types and the male and females roles that we have learnt to play. The strength of a man is in his presence. The strength of a woman is in her vulnerability. As women experience the cycles of nature with each passing month, men honour, adore, love and support all of it. Because women are our queens. Both men and women show their courage by stepping into their strengths. Valence vanishes and we see men and women for the purity that they are. It is love that grants access to the barriers that layer our hearts. When we honour our excitement in each other's presence, intimacy becomes inevitable. Romance takes a new dimension that is beyond the wet fantasies that are projected by men and women.

When we no longer fear our sexual energy, we become sexually expansive. We do not resist arousal. We allow the sexual energy to hyper-charge our hearts. Penetration is no longer a race to reach climax. Our sexual charge propels us beyond our senses. Each breath becomes engulfing. Each touch, charged with eminence, each whisper ecstatic. When we look into their eyes, we see past who they think they are. Identity disappears and we become suddenly infinite. We recover traces of memories that remind us of the source beyond this life. It is through love that nature intended new life to be born. The euphoria of love charged with the fire of creativity. The sexual impulse to create undresses the cloak of withheld potential. A creative explosion in our heart gives purposeless direction. It matters not the path we take because erotic potency magnifies our desirability for this moment. We break the boundaries we said we would not cross—the panic zone in the distant past—because there are moments in life where the only possible option is to lose all control. We lose our well-held balance so that our lover sees all of us. We do not hold back on love because this moment is forever. We are seen in all our light! Because we are not playing with each other's minds, our playground suddenly becomes much bigger. Our senses vanish from existence and we enter a sacred union: a merging of a spiritual dimension, much deeper than the physical. We enter a mysterious communion of two who become one to reincarnate the omnipresent. We feel strength beyond measure because all that was protecting us from good and evil acquires a mysterious innocence. We are reminded of a kind of purified madness. We have entered the realms in which we refused to go because to venture into the unknown would render the world we know nonsensical. Then, as we lie there, stripped naked of our flaws, we let go of our well held balance of the world because the world is not as we thought it would be. We return to our lives with a force of love that is beyond the point of no return. It is in moments of such power that we realise we have just begun.

Flow in Nature

What is it to be a man who knows nothing of his land? The man who knows not the directions the birds fly before nightfall. The man who knows not which animal trails lead to which food source. The man who knows not which root structure extracts which nutrients.

Security exists not with men who fill their pockets and mow their lawns on Sunday mornings. A well-groomed garden proves little of our power over nature. Security comes from men who know the songs of the plants and dances of the creatures. He understands his place alongside the guardians of the forest. Nature is not a walk through the forest. It is when we step truly into nature that we realise the extent to which society has put structures and systems in place, disabling us from our own nature. Society extracts the blood of our ancestors from the very soil that we have become so distant to. The Great Mother does not hold back in fear that she may one day run out of oil. The Great Mother does not say the destruction is wrong. She simply provides all that her children ever dreamt of.

We find that when we spend time with the Great Mother, her presence, the attention that she so generously gives brings us to our own presence. It is this presence that allows us to commune with flowers. The flower offers us beauty so that we experience the beauty within ourselves. The caribou stag talks of leadership. The great stag lures the hunters by standing proud with his magnificent antlers. He draws the hunters away from his herd, away from his children. The stag is a king who cares for the prosperity of his herd and protects it with his own life. The black jaguar talks of humility. Despite her power, she does not draw attention to herself. She is invisible amongst the branches of the trees. Humility is knowing when to use our strength. The chimpanzees patrol the forest with its troop. The clash with other tribes is sometimes violent. The chimpanzee speaks to us about greed. No matter how much the troop defends its territory, the seasons always change. The troop migrates to a new location where they find it more welcoming. No amount of control can prevent change. Like all else that exists in nature we cannot be controlled. We do not buy what is already ours. The land that we stand on. The water that we drink. The air that we breathe. The fire that gives us energy.

Our wildness cannot be masked by morals and values imposed by those whose beliefs are based on fear. Yet collective fear organises the laws of the land, the allocation of education, the values of resources, the structure of the economy and the prosperity of the people. Our power remains in our wildness. Wildness treats every moment as a ceremony. Because we have departed from nature, we require ceremony and daily rituals to connect us to what is true, to return to the source. When we work lifelessly for that which we have been led to do, it weakens us. This is what we do on our weekdays—our weak days.

Ceremony exists in that which we are eternally grateful for. To prepare a meal, we gather the wood that will make fire and chop it into smaller pieces. We light the kindling and it warms our hearts to see the fire turn into coal. We put on the flame the pot we have made out of the same clay in which our food grows. We add water into the pot. It softens the potatoes we have dug out with our hands. We energise the flame with air to keep it burning. It is the union of all these elements that creates ceremony. Through ceremony, we honour our Great Mother and thank her for answering our prayers. It is through ceremony that we draw our strength, the strength that comes from all the elements working in unity. We do not flow in Nature. Nature flows through us. Let us not forget who we are.

Flow in Synchronicity

The inward journey is that of becoming nothing because nothing is always greater than something. It is through complete non-attachment that we find what everyone is looking for: love. The kind of love that is, by its very nature, unconditional; the state where our mind's attention is absorbed completely by our own hearts. The full absorption into nothing is love of the highest order. When we find love, we have nothing more to gain. Instead the more we give, the more we get. What we get back is ultimately, love.

Once the inward journey is complete, it is time for the outward journey to being, that of synchronicity, that of co-creation. This is when love begins to emanate in everything we do. We find that the frequency of synchronicity begins to multiply dramatically. The prevalence of synchronicity is an indicator of our alignment with a higher order. Love demands non-attachment; as such all resistance ceases to exist. The external no longer has any power over us. We are freed from avoiding the inevitable. We simply change as the heart desires. Like the wind that suddenly changes direction, we do so without ever having to explain why. The full alignment with the higher order clears all resistance in our path. Our unimpeded flow gains the momentum of ceaseless synchronicity. As we welcome the unforeseen schedules of divine order, our path saturates with synchronicity. Then, there is no need to define our path. To do so would limit the multidimensional possibilities that are available to us in this moment. This is the intelligence of the unknowable.

We find that life becomes excessively difficult the moment we divert from our heart. A business deal may fall through, a friendship may become toxic, and a lifestyle may lose meaning. All these misfortunes are signposts pointing in the direction of our freedom. To become the everlasting presence of the freest of all states: the God state. With identity completely vaporised by love, we work simultaneously in multiple locations and periods of time. We gain true nonlinearity. Possibility materialises in the moment because we are the possibility and simultaneously become it. Because speed is distance divided by time, the nature of timelessness nulls the distance to our goals. End and means are one. We are accelerated to God speed.

In the God state we have access to higher realms of intelligence. These arrive precisely at the required moment. A moment sooner or later will render the possibilities out of alignment. Therefore, there is no such thing as sooner or later. The intelligence is only relevant to the moment. Without plans and schedules, our timing becomes immaculate. With material desires lacking meaning, the true nature of our potential is revealed. The God state is the embodiment of copious amounts of love. Each moment is in devotion and service to the expansion of consciousness that is beyond human intellect. Our purity grants access to the gifts of the higher realms. Gifts that are intangible in comprehension yet are undeniably potent. We no longer doubt the existence of the spirit realms. It is synchronicity that evokes magic.

UN-ECLIPSED - STORY OF EMBODYING OUR PROPHECY

The moon is silver. Whitewolf is 14 as he stands in front of his classmates ready to receive an award that granted him a scholarship to the best music school in the country. It is exactly this scholarship that Whitewolf is repelled by. He does not need someone telling him how to play music. Music is his freedom!

No school is going to pollute his mind. Instead of school he will busk. His music is a fight against the darkness he was born in. When he was six weeks old, he was removed from his mother because of her mental instability. His father had abused his mother. He was a child born out of violation. He busks near a skate park in a small town in Northern New South Wales, Australia. His grungy music has a powerful influence on the skateboarders who are also rebelling against the system. One of the skateboarders feels so inspired by his music that he gives him his own skateboard. That night Whitewolf skates down the dusty street when a car without headlights runs into him. Whitewolf walks away with his head hemorrhaging; he is losing dangerous amounts of blood. This does not deter Whitewolf. Tonight he is going to play at the local pub.

Whitewolf walks on stage with his t-shirt soaked in blood amidst a huge roar from the kids who look up to their victor. Whitewolf begins to play his music with a fury of passion. For four hours he plays with a marsh pit of rebels. Then suddenly everything goes black. Whitewolf collapses with blood splashing everywhere; the sight frightens some, others run on stage to help. Whitewolf is crowd-surfed to the exit. The stage manager weeps as she says, 'If there is no Whitewolf, there is no music.' Whitewolf hears her voice and says, 'If there is no music, there is no Whitewolf'. The ambulance arrives minutes later.

A hospital is no place for a wolf. He darts from it the moment no one is watching. Back on the streets the kids celebrate him. It is then that Whitewolf sees that music is so much bigger than he is. Music is no longer an escape from the adversities of his own life. Music is his gift to the world. Whitewolf gives himself to service beyond need. This is no longer about him. He will sing for the people to come into their power. And for the people he sang.

Whitewolf starts to travel the country with his music. He is attracted to places where fires are lit under the moon. He finds himself amongst the elders of indigenous communities deep in the desert lands of Australia. The indigenous grant him the wisdom of the wallaby, the jokes of the kookaburra and the trickery of the serpent. There is truth in ancient wisdom yet Whitewolf is the embodiment of truth itself. He yells out to country, 'I don't care about what I want to sing, I want to know what you want to sing. Sing through me. Sing your song.'

Whitewolf's music travels that land. On one stormy weekend, he finds himself in a rowdy bar. His intuition tells him not to play the songs that he knows. He begins to improvise and an energy starts to pulse through his body. He begins to scream louder and the crowd responds with just as much fire. Whitewolf slips into a daze. His subconscious takes over the music as he sees visions of the land. The spirit of country speaks to him. His prophecy is revealed to him; a door is opened from truth. He sees himself playing his music in front of millions of people but this is no ordinary crowd. This is a crowd of Aztecs: the keepers of ancient wisdom. He feels that wisdom flowing through him. The truth purifies his presence, which in turn liberates the millions from the weight of space and time. Whitewolf sings for hours. When he wakes up from his trance he notices that the whole pub is silent. As he gets off stage, a man who was cheering at the front approaches him. He asks, 'What did you just do?' 'I gave myself to the land for her to sing through me,' replies Whitewolf.

The following week Whitewolf arrives in Sydney. He plays at sold-out events around the city. At one of his concerts he talks about sharing his music with the world. After his performance, a DJ approaches him and offers to buy him a ticket to America where he can record his music with producers who have worked with celebrity musicians. Whitewolf does not hesitate to take the offer. He flies to the U.S. and produces three songs. The producers ask him to aim his music to a greater audience and enter the pop genre. Money does not tell Whitewolf what to do. His prophecy speaks of far greater intentions. That night Whitewolf is invited to play at a gathering in Mexico. An indigenous Grandmother pays for his ticket. Two days later Whitewolf is surrounded by 400 Aztecs, the tribes united by the beats of the enormous drums. The Grandmother then asks Whitewolf to perform. Whitewolf reaches for his guitar, but as he does, the Grandmother tells him he won't need it. Whitewolf picks up two drums sticks and steps up on stage. An energy charges through his body, a surge so strong that he feels his muscles magnify in strength. His body suddenly becomes far bigger than he thought was possible.

He begins to pound the drum with the strength of a thousand men. He screams 'AY YANA AY'. The Aztecs absorb his strength and multiply it by 400 before reflecting it back to him. Whitewolf slips into another trance. His screams become frequencies that are embedded with intelligence. His voice travels through the Aztecs like a new piece of code that reprograms the subconscious. Some cry, some shout and some tremble uncontrollably, each person heightened into a state of purity. Whitewolf notices none of this. He is in a trance of his own. He hallucinates visions that are from the realm of spirits and these visions are coded into his songs.

After what seems like several days, Whitewolf awakes from his trance. The Aztecs endow him with flowers. His visions guide him back to Sydney. Within a week of arriving, hundreds of people from all walks of life gather together in song. Each person feeling as the Aztecs did. Their subconscious reprogrammed through sound. Their spirits elevated and their intentions gaining profound clarity. A movement begins. Tribes unite. The masses awaken. The people are empowered by the liberty to speak their own truth. Their former lifestyle loses relevance as their intentions are no longer about themselves. Many strengthen in their service to community. Some awaken gifts they had never known.

Meanwhile, Whitewolf who is 21 years of age, advises industry leaders. He speaks with ministers of governments. He speaks with those at the forefront of food and energy, his words potent with a message aligned with divine law. His messages, visions and intentions come from the purity of the freest state of man, the God state.

★ ★ ★

It is through complete surrender that we find complete freedom. Surrender allows us to become a clear channel for intelligence to flow through us. It is our purity that intelligence is attracted to. We realise our prophecy when we access the God state. Without the God state, our intentions are limited to a reality defined by concepts of space and time. We do not fear our own power! Instead we are in reverence of each person we encounter because they too enter this state. No illusion can withstand purity. There is no darkness. There is only absence of light. The brave are forgiven because they dared to follow their heart. Despite the temptations of money, power and greed, they accepted their prophecy.

Part Three

Fathomless Magic

This part of the book looks at possibilities beyond the mind-derived realities of time and space. By experiencing the supernatural, we demystify that which makes our reality nonsensical. We find that magic becomes our reality.

The 7 Principles of Magic

1. Magic asks us to forget everything that we know.

2. Magic cannot be learnt. Magic reveals itself as required by the moment.

3. Magic can only be performed from altered states.

4. Magic can not be used in service of ourselves or others, magic is in service of Love itself.

5. It is purity that grants us access to magic. Light, the purest state of Love. Truth, the purest vibration of thought.

6. We do not explain magic.

7. It is purity that protects us from any energies that have been misaligned or tries to control us.

Prayer of the Heart

I never really cared for
the things of this world
It was the glow of your presence
that filled it with beauty

~ Hafiz

When we fall in love, we become like children. Life is not serious. Love is made of sunlight and chocolate bars.

It happens suddenly, when we least expect it. We meet someone. This one's different. They have a light inside their eyes. That magical thing happens between two people when they are young and everything is about to change. We do not yet know which direction to take but we take the risk. We tell them intimate things and hope they will still love us. We feel that our love is so strong, no force can keep us apart. Then if we don't hear from them, our world crumbles; death seems an easier option than a moment longer without them. What is the distance between us when we are in love and what is the distance when there are words unspoken? Some may try to close this distance by doing things by hand. They might handwrite a letter or build their lover a coffee table. This is how they show how much they love the other when words fail. And because we are young, career is important otherwise no one will notice us. We take the job that drains the magic from each day. We come home, too exhausted to look into each other's eyes. The light in their eyes no longer reminds us why we met and why we fell in love. We tell ourselves that we are not good for each other. It might be easier seeing other people. After all, love is a binary choice we make when we notice someone.

A few dates later, we become cautious. The last relationship demanded more from us than we were prepared for. It made us rethink who we are. We do not want to step into another relationship, not just yet. Even though our bed is half-empty, we become slightly unavailable. There are a few things to figure out before we know ourselves enough to be with someone. For some, the inability to accept themselves means that they spend their lifetime waiting for the right person to appear. They spend their whole life preparing to be loved just to meet someone who loves them for all the things they had prepared for. This kind of preparation leads us to fall in love with the ideas we have about someone. Perhaps it is ideas of wealth. Money may secure a relationship. But a relationship is not love. In fact many relationships end because of the unreasonable expectation of love. Everyone is looking for love. We may look for it in career, relationship or family. The unpleasant truth is that as long as we are looking for love we will not find it. Whatever we love will one day leave us. This is why we fear change. This is why despite what we love, we inevitably incur the fear of loss.

As long as we resist change we will be defeated. We forget that love is an adventure in which we are meant to lose ourselves. However, love does not ask us to be an adventurer nor a warrior. Love asks us to be both lost and broken. Through losing ourselves, we learn surrender. We surrender like the warrior who steps into battle, willing to lose what they love the most. We cannot take away something from someone who has nothing left. When we are utterly alone we overcome the most feared moment of our existence. By surrendering to death, we have already won the most important battle of our life. The battle that we have fought without end. The battle with ourselves. We do not need someone to completely accept us. We accept ourselves completely. It is then that we realise that Love is the answer that we refused to accept.

Devotion

When we surrender to love, we find immunity from change. When we have lost interest in the outcome, love cannot hurt. Love is no longer dependent on anything that is outside us. Love is not what we need. Love is what we are. The love that erupts out of our hearts like a volcanic fountain of warmth, this love comes from falling in love with our first date: the universe that is within us. Because we surrendered in the darkest moment when death came knocking on our door, each moment ever since reminds us that we are alive. Because we exist, we do not avoid life. To honour our own existence is a tremendous act of love. Because we are alive, we honour our life by living all that we ever dreamt of. Love favours the brave. When life falls in love with us, death thinks twice about its purpose. We honour our existence through devotion. We do everything that brings us closer to our heart.

This is the woman who leaves her husband to find herself. To reunite with the power that she knows to be no less than magic. She loves to sing, yet it is the enchantment of her own voice that she has become distant to. She has been approached by record labels asking her to sing pre-written songs that would bring her great wealth. Yet she didn't resonate with anything the labels asked of her. She was born with a resonance of her own. A resonance that made her uncomfortable singing words that did not come from her own heart. After leaving her husband, she opens the song book, which she had made out of magazine cuttings when she was eleven. Each picture symbolised a feeling that she had and she would sing about this feeling. It is through feeling that her mind would disappear. Only through feeling did her heart speak, uninterrupted. Only through feeling were her words pure. Only through feeling did her songs melt the hearts of those around her. She looks at the pictures in her song book. Her feelings have changed. Her heart sees a picture of a magnificent meadow with a single tree. The tree with two golden birds on one of its arms, she also spots a frog clinging to the trunk, a rabbit hopping about in the meadow and a butterfly hovering over a turtle. The memories of her childhood merge with the elegance of her experience. She sings of the little children of the tree, the children who have no opinion—not even of themselves. She sings of the space that is created when opinion departs this world. She sings of the space filled by love, a love present in each of the tree's children. As she rediscovers herself in song, she begins to cry. Each tear removes a layer of the veil that clouded her heart. With each tear, the sparkle in her eyes becomes brighter. She cries the tears that she refused to show when she was with her husband. She cries because her heart is still broken. She cries to keep her heart open.

It is through tears that we prevent the heart from closing prematurely. When the heart has cried all that it needs, there is nothing left to protect our heart. The entity of fear no longer protects us. Love does. Because love is unconditional, we find immunity to hurt. We no longer fear change. It is through devotion that our heart finds strength.

Love becomes our primary purpose. All else is secondary. It is through love that we heal. Our intentions are of the highest order because they are not based on decisions made by subconscious entities that have become visceral. The mind no longer has answers, the heart no longer has questions. Brain and body are in complete harmony. With our hearts flooded by a tsunami of love, our arteries begin to pump this love into every cell of our body, each organ replenished by the affection it always longed for. It is through devotion that we ignite the flame in our heart. The eternal source of love. Blessed we are, for it is the heart of men that contains the love of the universe.

Compassion

With our hearts open, our natural impulse is to be kind. It does not matter what our identities lead us to believe, love treats us all the same. We only fool ourselves by trying to impress others. Love crosses all boundaries. Boundaries have divided nations, they separate the rich and the poor, and tear apart our people who are both black and white. What is it to be human in a land made of boundaries? Boundaries create walls within ourselves.

Because we cannot live this moment again, this is our one chance to be kind. We do not hold back on love because this moment is forever. Love is like wealth, the more we keep it to ourselves, the more lonely we get. So we love each other fiercely! Our love is pure because it does not come from anything external, it lacks motive. We love, to honour our gift: the miracle of life.

Our love comes from the purest of sources. We do not have judgment because each judgment is an entity. The entity speaks when it sees itself in another. The entity is triggered by what it has experienced before. The entity reacts to anything that allows it to be seen. Judgment is therefore how we see ourselves. When we love, we lose all fear of being seen. We bless another with our presence. We are in reverence of witnessing God in one another. We are treated the way we treat ourselves. We sacrifice everything for the purity of love. What we sacrifice is, ultimately, illusion. There is nothing more powerful than when our presence takes away the words from the one before us.

A young father has seen the ones who pray for all the things he takes for granted. His heart is no longer his. His love is the single flame that shines from a thousand candles. One day, as he walks to the preschool to pick up his son, he instinctively runs towards a ball that is about to roll onto a busy road. When we become a father, we seem to gain an extra sense. The young child witnesses the urgency of this compassionate act. When the child returns home, he too runs to help his older brother who is dragging a heavy log to build a secret hutch. The young father arrives at the preschool to pick up his son. His little sunshine complains that an older boy has been bullying him. The father asks the young bully to come with them. He leads them to a nearby ice-cream vendor. He buys both children ice-cream and then takes them to a nearby playground where he plays on the swings with both of them. The young bully laughs with the boy he was jealous of. The bully had not yet learnt to engage with other kids his age. All he wanted was to play with the other kids. But he felt hostility from them because when we are left out, we see everyone as hostile. The young bully and the young boy become inseparable friends. Their friendship sets an example of unity amongst the kids in the preschool.

Because we love, life gives back more of what we have. Our purity shines through all that is seen on the surface. On the surface, an office clerk is annoyed by the hardship of working long hours. When he enters the supermarket, he forcefully pushes past an old woman who is slow and her body is reminding her that life will soon come to an end. The old woman sees the clerk deeper than his aggression. She does not question where the aggression comes from. She calls after the office clerk. She tells him that the woman on the second counter has a crush on him. She gives him five dollars of her own money to buy a box of chocolate and leave it with her when he leaves the counter. The office clerk is broken out of his internal commotion as he listens to the old woman. He had never noticed the woman at the counter before but now that he looks at her, he finds her mysteriously attractive. Then his life crisis returns back to his head and he impatiently thanks the old woman and goes about selecting his groceries. He mindlessly forgets about the woman at the counter. A few weeks later, he walks on the sidewalk and finds the woman at the counter getting out of her car at the service station. She is approached passionately by a man who is in the car behind hers. The office clerk feels an unexpected surge of envy. The crisis of his life returns to him. His anger drives him to accidentally bump into a passerby. The passerby pushes him away with just as much aggression. The office clerk is reminded of the old woman that he had pushed past at the supermarket. He is suddenly filled by compounding humility. He does not react to the passerby. He cannot help but be humbled by the compassion of the old woman. It is love that allows us to dance with this eternal moment.

Sometimes we may find that our love is not returned. We love anyway because love was never an exchange. Love is like the rain; it does not water some trees and leave out others. Because our love lacks motive, we do not say that I am yours and you are mine. We simply love because it is the heart's desire to connect us all. Because we have been lost and we have been broken, we have learnt that without the warmth of love, our hearts begin to decay. So we devote ourselves to love without end. Love can never fail us because the source of our strength is surrender. The wounded make powerful healers because the lack of love has taught them that fire can be lit even when the night is dark and the kindling is wet. Because we get to know ourselves though those who love us, it is worth the risk. Because we can't help falling in love, we love without a choice in the matter. Our hearts never skipped a beat because one day they were tired. It is love that has been knocking on the doors to our heart, from the very start.

Intention

When love becomes our first priority, nothing else seems to matters anymore. All our responses come from surrendered action. With love inside, we become utterly free of defense. The surrendered have already won because there is nothing left to lose. It is then that we find true freedom from desire. Because we already have what everyone seeks (love), our desire lacks the prize of reward. The illusion of reward is the real obstacle to what we desire. Because we do not seek in lack, we become immune to disappointment. Since change is inevitable, what we seek lacks motive. Therefore we simply set our intention and let go of the outcome. Then we find the courage to desire that which we have been conditioned not to.

The young law student considers herself lucky to find an internship at the prosecutor's office. As she reviews the cases of each of the offenders, she becomes aware of the insanity of preparing offenders for more crime. A criminal record means that the offenders would be less likely to find a new job, they would be rejected by community and are more likely to repeat that which started them on a path of crime. She speaks of her concern to her superiors. Her superiors speak to her of other important matters. The young student is not so easily fooled. Without fear she points out to her supervisors that they are diverting her attention to avoid the issue. Her supervisors threaten her with the risk of losing her job if she continues to argue with what she is told. The young student takes surrendered action. She tells her superiors that she will stay in her internship, only if they consider her ideas. Her supervisors reject her offer and the young student loses her job. She spends weeks looking for another internship and finally gets an interview at the criminal justice office. In her interview, her superiors ask her why she wants this job. The young student talks of the injustice that she sees. She talks of prevention rather than prosecution. She talks of giving the offenders the option of community service, an option that would allow them to reintegrate back into the community. The criminal justice office admires the depth of her insight. They see that the young student is not looking for a job just for the money. They take her up on her ideas and ask her to start an entirely new department. One that will change the role of prosecutors from having all the power, to one of giving power back to the offenders so they have the opportunity to redeem themselves. The young student leads the new department humbled by the trust of her superiors. The older staff admire the young student for being brave amongst leaders who sometime give up on speaking up. Through surrendered action, she finds alignment with her intentions.

Surrendered action allows us to stay on a path that is far greater than any we can ever imagine. We become easily distracted and impatient with that which denies the heart of love. This simply means that there is something calling our heart to deepen our love. Far too often we regret that when love called us, we did not answer. When we follow the irresistible urge of our hearts, we find that we become a magnet for magic. Love attracts synchronicity because Angels are captivated by pure beings. Because our heart's desire is inseparable from this moment, we are wholeheartedly committed to the steps we can take now. When we accept the path that burns in our heart, our path begins to run towards us, to greet us in our every step. By simply playing our part, we allow others to love us. Surrender is our greatest strength and as such, it is our greatest act of love. Money, power and greed become temptations too small for a surrendered heart. Then, when death knocks on our door, we do not fight for a life un-lived, but welcome death as an old friend.

Connection

Love is a language that everyone understands. Differently. For some love is whispered when no one's watching, for some love is written on a discarded piece of paper, for some love is affection expressed through touch, for others love is the number of times they are remembered in a day. Some may show love by not reacting, for others a reaction is what tells them that they are loved.

When we are in love, we find a place in our lover's diary. This diary holds moments of utter joy, each note written in honour of our hopes and dreams together. This diary seeks to find out what makes our lover's tick, but its pages are ripped and burnt when we decide to look the other way. Then there are days when a lesson is learnt, a lesson that comes from the accumulation of light wounds because what doesn't kill us, makes us stronger. This is what we think until one day we find out that a third party was involved, a person who was not in the original script. The notes we wrote each time we remembered our lover are quickly forgotten. How easily does love escape from us when doubt consumes the mind. Those emotions that sabotage our behaviour surprise even us. Those who return to love write in their diary that wounds must be healed through forgiveness the moment they are made. The past is to be forbidden from any future retaliation. Then we see that love never forgets us; we forget love. Love is immeasurable, yet the depth of the heart can be comprehended by how much we can forgive.

As long as a relationship is based on the mutual lack, emotions are an invitation for dialogue. However, no amount of emotions will bring us closer to someone's heart in the absence of love. Emotions can be like the clouds that block the light from the sky; or they can be the infinite stars that bring light to the night. We find that we come together as lovers because there is yet much to discover about our own hearts. Then, when we are finally consumed by the love within ourselves, our emotions are devoured whole by the purest of sources. That love allows us to take greater emotional risks because love is free and cannot be controlled by our will. The White Magician has faced battles both mystical and in flesh. Each challenge propels him in the direction of love. The White Magician walks amongst common men yet little do they know of the power he possesses. The White Magician's sorcery lacks motive because nothing is ever his and he has nothing to gain. He is already complete; there is nothing left to need. There is no longing, yet he has seen her looking and he knows that she is coming. One frosty evening when there is little to do, there are three knocks on his cottage door. It is her. What if he does not answer? He waits, but there are no more knocks. To be sure, he waits a little more before he opens the door. There she is, waiting at his doorstep.

'I'm sorry, I didn't know if you were home,' she says from under her silver cloak. She walks inside without being invited and the White Magician closes the door behind them. She says that she is here to find the passage of the pilgrim. The White Magician knows that life brings two people together for reasons they do not yet know of. How can he be sure if she is the one?

'I know someone who can help you,' says the White Magician. He notices the fickle disappointment in her eyes, one that is only visible to those who speak to their soulmate's heart. 'The pilgrim's path does not lead to paradise. Take the narrow road to where the river divides, you will find the monastery when the 7th star of the Pleiadians is at its brightest,' the White Magician suggests. He then opens the door and gestures for her to leave.

The pilgrim's journey takes many years. In her journey, she learns of heartbreak from men who see her as no more than an object to be had. She learns of liberating her emotions by dancing under the moonlight with women who care little about what others think of them. She learns of combining her playfulness with her womanhood in times when she is alone to speak with her own soul. It is the 11th moon of the year when she remembers the White Magician. All of a sudden she is drawn into fantasies about the White Magician she did not have before. She decides to return to thank him for guiding her on her path.

Ten years have passed since the White Magician last saw her. At his doorstep is a woman with great power. He boils some water with medicinal herbs to make a special tea.

'Do you want to know the secret of the pilgrim?' he asks.

She is slightly annoyed by the question. 'Why didn't you tell me the secret at the start of the journey?' she asks.

'You weren't ready then but you are here now. The pilgrimage teaches us to forget everything we have ever learnt to become spellbound by the moment we are experiencing right now.'

Love is a power so deep, we respect what we find. Love is the language of Angels, each word unraveling the secrets to our existence. We see the gift of sacred union that is not just of the heart, but ignites both body and mind. We connect mentally, physically, emotionally and sexually, all at once. The only love we defend is the love for ourselves. By loving ourselves, we love all. In this manner we restore faith in true love.

Take me Deeper - Story of soulmates

She had played many games at night, but there were only a few that she had decided to remember. With him though, it wasn't a game. Zara had seen him come down from the mountains at sunset. He would walk as if gliding on the sand so that no grain felt displaced. Sunsets at the Bamboo resort in Thailand were breathtaking. Yet he didn't seem like he was interested in the sunset itself. He came to commune with the invisible because it is at sunset that they come out to wander.

He still has not noticed her even though she was sitting directly opposite him at the restaurant the previous night. It is not too late. She will talk to him when he comes to the restaurant for breakfast the next morning. She deliberately sleeps in the next morning ignoring her plans to speak with him. She will go for a morning swim in the ocean and then find people to hang out with. She orders a green smoothie at the resort after her swim and is startled to see him sitting at the table beside her. Without thinking, she asks if he has a cable to charge her phone. What is she thinking? She does not even have her phone with her. A single word answer is all she receives. Is this the end of the conversation? Zara sits there, not knowing whether to leave him alone or say something else. She sees that his eyes see many things, except for her. She decides to leave him alone but her body does not move. In that moment, all of his attention falls on her. Paralysed by his eyes, Zara's heart starts pounding. Is this a warning sign for danger or is it her intuition telling her something? His smile comes from a place in his heart that instantly melts all her fears.

He talks of the quartz crystals in the sand that are worn out from the granite rocks, which make up the island. Zara isn't interested in understanding what sand is made of. Why is he telling her this? In fact, he too is just as nervous as her. Saying something devoid of emotion allows him to hide his own racing heart, the heart that tells him she is the one. His mind is still unconvinced that they are meant for each other. How do you make love last anyway?

'Let's take the boat this afternoon to the beach that has been abandoned,' he says flatly.

'I can see you here at 3:00,' she says.

The boat resembles a carved out canoe with an outboard that seems far too powerful for its purpose. The outboard is too loud for them to have a conversation. She looks to the endless horizon. He steers the boat like a man who directs his horse without command. Their canoe runs aground on the abandoned beach. Questions come into her mind. They are alone and she has only spoken with him once before. He anchors the boat in the sand and their footprints head towards the hollow in the sand where a river once flowed. They begin walking up the dried riverbed. Only the forest speaks as they ascend up the river path. He stops to point at a tree. 'See the subtle clearing in the branches? It is where the monkeys carve out their trails through the canopy.' His words do little to put Zara at ease. They reach the bottom of a granite cliff. He walks around the cliff and shakes off a rope that had been hidden by dead leaves. The rope was already fastened to something that Zara could not see from the bottom. 'Up you go,' he says.

She reluctantly grabs the rope and starts climbing, her fear escalating with the height. He climbs the rope after her and soon, they reach the top of the cliff. There, she finally sees why they have gone through all the effort. In front of her is a majestic cave overlooking the ocean. The enormity of the cave makes Zara feel like she is inside a cathedral of the earth. The granite walls of the cave twinkle with countless crystals embedded within it. Zara sits on a log admiring nature as he collects some firewood.

As the sun begins to descend towards the horizon, he takes her arm and they walk to the edge of the cliff. He stands behind her and spreads her arms out wide. He then lets out a loud roar that seems to upset the tranquility around them. 'Scream with me,' he says.

She looks at him slightly shy and slightly confused by the absurdity. He lets out another wild scream and she makes a weak attempt at screaming with him.

'Louder,' he says as he wildly shakes her body. It is then that she feels his strength. A strength that can protect her from all harm. For an instant, Zara forgets who she is and lets out a wild scream. He joins in and harmonizes with her voice.

'That felt so good,' she says.

'The shameless do not doubt,' he says. He releases her and stands next to her. 'It is when we are wild that we are truly free,' he says. They both scream like wild adolescent animals whose voices are just breaking. The sound is terrible, but liberating for this reason. He pulls her away from the cliff and they caress each other playfully, her skin bright as the clouds just after the sun has set, his eyes reaching deep into hers. They go to a place where the mind is unable to follow.

She penetrates his soul as she looks into his eyes. 'I feel like this moment is a wave that briefly appears in the ocean, only to be swallowed back into the infinite depths.' She pauses for a moment. 'But this is superficial. I can go deeper,' she says.

'Take me deeper,' he says.
I see in your eyes
Evidence of matters
Relating to the heart.
My senses are all confused
This insanity feels far more real
Than a world which has
Interfered with Magic
'Take me deeper,' she says
I see you better
When I close my eyes
You teleport me to another place
When you squeeze me tight
The place under the table
Where we hide as children
I share with you my shelter
The place where I love you
Together we treat each other
With the gifts we only know as kids
'Take me deeper,' he says
I love you
Because I have no reason
To be with you

You set me free
By taking away
All agendas
Agendas that speak of love
But never are
'Take me deeper,' she says
You offer me everything
By expecting nothing
Of me
Love pouring out of our hearts
There is nothing left to ask
Together we take a bath
In the waters of Love
'Take me deeper,' he says
You are the lighthouse
I stop running
The moment I see you
Your attention
The precious gift
That allows me to
Find my island
'Take me deeper,' she says
I see no end
To the love my heart
Has never known
The love that

Transforms sorrows
The universal elixir
That keeps love
Eternal
'Take me deeper,' he says
There isn't a day that passes
That I need
Without you there is no gift
That I may one day
Be needed
It is because I serve
That I love
'Take me deeper,' she says
I look out of the window
When it rains
Not because I wait for you
But because I'm sending
So much love your way
We love the fire more
On the days that it rains
'Take me deeper,' he says
'Enough,' she says
'I don't want to go any further.'

Zara is locked in an embrace she never wants to escape. Their dance enters the realm of the departed souls, a place where we go to recover moments of déjà vu, a place that reminds us where we have seen each other before, where love is beyond each individual. Their souls contemplate each other. She sees the stars behind his eyes. He sees the wings of her heart soaring in the sky. Her soul informs him that she is not ready yet. That he must wait. That she will test the bravery of his heart. His soul sees neither past nor future. He shows her nothing of the predicament that he has just seen. They celebrate this moment that dissolves lifetimes of waiting.

The first rays of the sun greets them by kissing their bare skin. Who better to remind you that today is a new day than the one beside you. Zara sits up, the soft sunlight carrying the magic of the night. He stands up without looking at her and walks to the edge of the cliff. For a moment she feels complete. The completeness you find in the hearts of butterflies that are intoxicated with the scent of flowers that welcome us into spring. They get dressed and slowly float down the dry riverbed. The sound of the canoe is a welcomed noise in the silence between them. They return to the Bamboo resort. He says that he has to return back in to the mountains. She says she will take the boat to the pier. Her flight to Vietnam is tomorrow morning and she must not be late for the airport.

As he walks up the mountain, she calls behind him. 'How will I find you, I don't even know your name,' she says with a trace of fear in her voice. 'Don't be afraid. As long as you follow your heart, the angels will always light your way,' he replies.

★ ★ ★

Love has never failed us. It has never been a mistake. We do not reason with love because love attracts what cannot be found. Each time we are lost, love is what we seek.

The Rewards of Risk

Life is a risk

~ Carmelo Anthony

We may never know our destiny. However to deny the calling of the heart would be a crisis of faith. As with all matters of the heart, the odds may not be in our favour but it is the only risk worth taking.

When we honour ourselves, now becomes the most exciting time to be alive. We have been granted the gift of creation that magically transforms dreams into reality. As creator, we are responsible for our own dreams. We do not create in the future, nor in the past. The magic of creation is only possible through the intelligence of this moment. As such, the biggest risk we take in our life is avoiding our dream in this moment in the hope that it may one day come true. We may fail many times over, true, but those who refuse to fail are yet to discover their dream. A dream that no one else can imagine.

We may avoid risk in favour of dying a comfortable death. Yet, the only comfort we may get from death is from a life where we risked it all. So we live at the edge of reality. Flirting with the unknown, we don't know what our dreams are anymore. Teasing the boundaries between the real and the imagined, death begins to keep its distance because we are protected by the mysterious forces that make our life difficult when we strayed from what is true to our hearts.

What do we prevent ourselves from desiring? The entities that live in the subconscious would suggest that the world will always exist with both the light and the dark. The end of darkness would mean the end of duality. What holds us back from embodying light alone? What hypothesis do we invent to defend darkness? Darkness exists as long as we give it meaning.

Without a source of income, his only choice is to look for work. But he doesn't. In fact with his expertise if he did apply for a job, he would most likely get it. This is exactly why he did not invest anytime in cover letters that mean little to him. In his heart he knows that he is lying to himself. He knows his purpose but not his path. There are nights when he walks to the only tree on the hill top of the neighbourhood park. No one will approach him there. In these moments he sits down and weeps hopelessly. He pleads with the invisible to give him a sign, to give him some direction. Because he has discovered his gift, he cannot return to the life he once knew. He grieves the life that he left behind. The life that provided money, recognition and security. He grieves the friends that he has lost because his heart rejected what they used to share. He grieves the future that he had once dreamt of. He weeps because he has lost the ability to retaliate. The entities of hurt and pain no longer exist in him and so are never triggered even by those who insult him. He weeps because it was easier being weak and betray love. There are innumerable events in his life where he has spontaneously performed that which he cannot explain. Far too many incidences which do not allow him to simply dismiss magic as imaginary. He has come too far. There is no turning back. He looks up to the cityscape before him, each floor, in each building, perpetuating the illusion of existence. He does not know his path, yet he cannot deny the mysterious force that has supported his journey in ways unimagined. His heart has led him places that no amount of planning would be able to recreate. In this moment, he feels blessed to be loved, despite how little money he has in his pocket. He thanks the mysterious forces that ask more of him than the mundane existence. He may not know where tomorrow leads, but tomorrow is inseparable from the choices he makes now. And in this moment he chooses love.

Even when we don't have the resources, we still step towards our dreams. We do not have to do it all alone. We ask for assistance. We ask because our dreams are never our own. As such, no one individual knows the plan woven in the divine fabric. The flow state is our baseline, propelling us forward with surrendered action. We enter collective flow when our hearts align with the incomprehensible. It is together that we enter the untapped realms where our plans are a singularity. The plan that knows no harm, no destruction. The plan that is worth risking everything for.

By not following our heart's desire, we prevent ourselves from living. The further we are from our dreams, the more we struggle with our lives. The one who struggles against their heart and the one who follows their heart both face challenges. However, for the one who follows their heart, their dreams are a little closer each time they surrender. Surrendering opens the gate for Angels to work with us on our dreams. Angels only speak to those who are true to their heart. They work together for the divine plan to unfold and surround those who share the remarkable gift of love. The kind of love that gives the courage for blind trust. Angels ask us to take the leap; they tell us that the trust part will come later. Trust comes from taking risks.

In times of great despair, we pray to all gods in existence. Then why not commune with the invisible when we are abundant? The existential crisis is the great dilemma of the living. We celebrate the miracle of our birth. Then what? Why do we need reasons for our own existence? What are our hopes, dreams, visions and intentions? Perhaps more generically, what are our thoughts and where do they come form? How do we know that our thoughts are our own?

Without a master, the mind becomes self-serving. The deeper we find ourselves in intellect the more isolated we feel. Our chronic thinking traps us in fear driven risk assessments and we forget to live. The more we invest in the mind, the more illusion we will find. There is no point investing in illusion.

The bystander asks the girl waiting to board a train, where she is going?

The girls says 'where my heart leads me.' The bystander says that the girl is much too young to be talking like that and must listen to her parents who are wiser. The girl replies that she cannot remember her parent's faces. She was raised by her grandmother who died two years ago. Before closing her eyes for the last time, her grandmother said to her, 'What you need to know, you will find inside.' The bystander says that you have little money and no place to stay, how will you survive?' The girls says, 'In the last 5 days, I have been welcomed inside a palace, feasted on a 7 course meal, slept under the bridge and shared my only meal of the day with street kids. I do not know where my heart is taking me but I keep falling in love with every moment given to me.' The bystander takes a moment to think. 'Each year he has worked harder and the cost of living has gone higher. The amount of wealth he has is always equivalent to the amount of debt he is in.' He turns to the girl and says, 'Time has not favoured me. I am much too old to be young and free. There will be a time when through my eyes you will see.' The girl places her hand on the heart of the bystander and asks '…and what will I see?' The bystander sees his entire life flash before his eyes. Suddenly it is not debt that is important anymore. His most treasured memories are of the woman who loved him more than anything and he loved her too. All they wanted to do was to be with each other. However, pain appeared when they were not paying attention to their own feelings. Pain told them stories and began to shape every moment they shared ever since. They fought over the details of the stories pain was telling them. As miserable as they were, he loved even the times they were mad at each other because at least they were together. But the more she loved him, the more he would push her away, saying that he did not want to hurt her. When he was without her, he would spend the days curled up in bed, waiting for time to end. Then, in moments of desperation, he would contact her to retell the stories of pain. Then one day he does not hear from her. Weeks, months, years pass by. Her last words clearly imprinted in his mind 'I don't know what to do to be good enough for you.' No matter how many ways she tried, she could not find her way to his lost heart. He forgot who he was the day he started believing in the stories pain was telling him. The bystander still listens to the stories of pain. It is through this pain that he advises others not to follow the desires that they have in their hearts. The girls sees tears in the bystanders eyes. The tears that well from emotions so deep that all thought is momentarily suspended. The girl moves away from the bystander without a word. Her train will soon arrive. Words fail to have meaning when we are truly seen. Only pain wishes to discuss.

What is the biggest risk that we can take? It is when we know for certain that we back ourselves. Such risk taking can become pathological when the stories we tell ourselves becomes self-serving. It takes enormous effort to defend our illusions. The enormity of our righteousness is equivalent to how lost we are. Fear makes everything overwhelming and our life becomes a gamble. We get caught up in what we wish for and the doubts we believe in. The moment we accept that we are lost and we do not know anything, the righteousness that was responsible for the crisis of faith forgets its purpose. When there are no parts of us left to interfere with the messages, we hear them clearly. Some may call this insights, epiphanies, creativity or imagination. Others speak of it as the whispers of Angels that we may hear at train stations. We do not know. We may never know if our thoughts are our own. It is then that we realise that when we are completely free, we are not controlled by our will. We may find that will power, ruthless confidence and righteousness only exist to convince ourselves and we may not know what is best for us. The intelligence of the heart is connected to all and therefore responds simultaneously in all locations and periods of time. When we listen to our hearts, it is never a risk. We listen because we often go against what we do not understand. We listen because what we know is not important. Our hearts are responsive to this moment so the miracles of communion are always precise, if it happens a moment sooner or a moment later, it would not be so. It is when we are constantly arriving that we never do. There are no more decisions because we do not discuss what we receive through communion. We take that step now because life is a constantly fleeting moment. We find that time becomes immaculate when the heart is no longer in a hurry.

We begin to reject certain things without knowing why. With love in our hearts, our subconscious is reprogrammed to the harmony of divine order. We find that what we reject restores the sacred glow back into our lives, the glow that is seen in people who have made many sacrifices because they do not wish to defend illusion anymore. Against all odds, we do not deceive ourselves of who we truly are. We do not give in to the governance that seeks to perpetuate illusion, the system that convinces us to become slaves of the economy. We wake up from the mechanisms that are there to control us. We risk everything to rise from the conditioning of our pre-appointed itinerary.

Flirting with Reality - Story of divine fortune

The miserable delinquent is asked to put on some sensible clothes and find work. Like the other kids, the delinquent sees little hope in the village. The village courtyard looks like a disaster zone. The old men always speak of the same things at the local pub and the history of the village has not changed much since the time of his grandfather. The delinquent sits on the banks of the misty lake and stares at the ripples made by the light breeze. He is suddenly alerted by the snapping of a twig behind him. He turns around to see an old man with a bushy white beard. The old man gestures to the boy to sit next to him. The delinquent gets up and starts walking away. 'I have no interest in strangers,' he says.

'I offer you the answers to the most important questions in your life,' the old man replies. The delinquent stops momentarily. 'In this bag is a small fortune, you have the option to take it and forever escape the injustices of your village or you can listen to what I have to say,' says the old man.

The boy looks at the bag with four gold coins. There is nothing that his village can offer him. They are all cowards consumed by self-pity and isolation. He reaches for the bag. The old man drops the bag in his hand and starts to walk away. In that instant the boy feels that something grave has happened and yells after the old man. 'Please wait. I don't want this gold. Please tell me what you know.'

The old man turns around and takes the bag from the boy and puts it back in his pocket. 'Do you trust me?' asks the old man.

'Who are you?' asks the boy.

'My name is Graessle the White Magician,' says the old man. 'Do you trust me?'

The boy nods.

'Will you do everything that I say,' asks Graessle.

'Yes,' replies the boy.

Graessle draws a large circle in the soil around them. He then says, 'Once you enter the circle there is no turning back.'

The boy hesitates but his body has already decided to carry him inside. Graessle lights a sacred fire within the circle and then recites some ancient mantras from a tradition that the boy does not recognise. The boy patiently sits in front of the fire as Graessle slips into a trance. The boy's body starts to shiver despite the heat from the fire. The boy had not experienced such tremor before. Graessle recites the mantra louder and louder as the mist from the lake engulfs the forest outside the circle. The boy begins to gag and cough violently. He does not know what is happening yet fear has long abandoned the journey.

'There is no holding back. Let it all out,' says Graessle.

The boy enters a deep trance and his body begins to spasm involuntarily. He screams and moans as he rolls uncontrollably on the ground. He does not care how much time has passed. He simply wants to do whatever it takes to end the torturous process. He begins to plead to the old man to stop. Graessle is unresponsive, deep in a trance of his own. The trembling begins to cease and the horror of the experience begins to fade with it.

Graessle then lights a dried tree branch. He calls upon the spirits of the land, angels and all forms of the divine to close the channels from which the boy's energy was being drained and to seal his aura and completely protect the boy from this moment on. The boy wakes up from a reality that seemed to predate the earth. He does not question what the old man did. His eyes have changed colour. His posture is different, his consciousness pure, the identity of his former self irrelevant. The light in his heart that was extinguished by the conditions he was born in, now burns fiercely.

'No more doubt. No more fear. Trust yourself and don't think that you are not good enough,' says Graessle. That is all that the boy wished to hear. Graessle then asks the boy to close the ceremony. The boy does not think, each word executed from an empty mind. He thanks the elements of the earth and all those who took part in the ceremony. The boy feels instilled with a strength that reminds him to never give up on love. The limits of the mind no longer setting barriers for the heart.

The boy returns to the village the next morning. A certain aura about him means that the villagers are drawn to something unusual. 'I have changed and I see the world differently now,' says the boy. An unerodable sense of peace follows him wherever he goes. The boy's presence robs the villagers of doubts and questions. It somehow takes more effort to defend their old identities than to let go of it.

'No one will be hungry today,' say the boy. 'Let's gather the fish from the lake, the wheat from the fields and the pots from our kitchens. We will have our first meal together.' The boy says this with a conviction so free of motive that no one is able to refuse. Some men go to the lake, others follow the children to the fields. The women gather together to collect flowers and dress up in their most beautiful gowns. By noon, the villagers return to the courtyard at the centre of the village. The men make a fire pit and the entire village cook together with joy and laughter, each villager empowered by their own autonomy. To this end, the boy is invisible until he speaks again.

'We do not learn how to live in harmony. It is the most natural thing. This way of existence is stolen from us when we are children. We are educated out of our gifts. We are asked to be sensible and do things that we have no interest in. From this moment on, we are in service to each other because we are all children of the Great Mother. I love you as I love myself. Let's honour our mothers and sisters for the care and support they gift us each day. For they inspire us to live a little better each day. For they listen to us even when all we talk about is ourselves. For they open the doors to our emotions and carry within them the hopes of our future.'

The boy looks deeply into the eyes of each woman in the courtyard. The brave souls without whom we would not know of things that silence our minds and melt our hearts. The boy speaks again.

'Let's honour our fathers and brothers for they work the fields in our honour. They love us even when they don't understand us. They speak little but make up for it with their actions. They are our companions when we do not wish to walk alone in the dark night. They never give up on love even when we reject them a thousand times.'

The boy pauses for a moment, his aura even brighter. He looks into the eyes of men who care for their children without ever needing an explanation.

'Let's share this meal in cerebration of ourselves and each other,' says the boy.

The men collect the plates and cutlery and the women fill their plates. The men hand the gift of sustenance, first to their children, then to the women. They all sit together. Forgotten are the shame and embarrassment we have around love and kindness. Each smile is received dearly, each offering of love, given generously.

As evening approaches, the boy sees that the children are instinctively finding purpose in what was seen before as trash. He sees that the women are decorating the courtyard with flowers, pebbles and branches. He sees the men repairing the long-neglected damage to the village courtyard.

He sees the village gaining the beauty that comes from appreciation. The boy finds that he is a single link in a chain of love that is circulating from heart to heart, replenishing the exuberance of each villager. The love of each person returned back to them, like all else that cycles in nature. As one cycle ends, another begins. The boy decides to leave the village and live as a journey man. The moon is silver and he shall call himself Whitewolf.

★ ★ ★

Let us not deny our earth, the beauty that it cries for. Let us not fear letting go of the systems that have enslaved us. Let us rise together in love and serve the hopes and dreams of each other. Let us trust the mysterious connection that returns us forever to this moment. If we consider the important questions in our lives, we may find that this was the plan all along.

Gift of Service

I fell asleep
and dreamt that
life was only happiness
I woke up and discovered
that life was service
I did my service
and discovered that
service was
Happiness

~ Paulo Coelho

When we trust easily and give willingly, we fall the hardest. Betrayal does not quiver us. We get back up and endure because it is the bonds that withstand the test of time that strengthen us. The best relationships are those based on mutual giving.

Being of service is entirely different from being a slave. It is by selling our soul that we become powerful, rich and beautiful. We become a slave to what we serve. We may be young and strong and always have food on our plate, yet when we grow old, we acquire other qualities. And if all we have invested in is self-enhancement, we find that we lose our power with time. As long as we give our power away, we live a life of bereavement. The only power that can be taken away from us is the one that we give. So we take it all back. We break the shackles that enslaved us. We stop pushing the massive rock of illusion up the mountain. We let the rock roll back down to the abyss from which it came. We use the strength we have gained from pushing the rock to climb up the mountain. Whichever road we have travelled, it has led us to this moment, where we walk amongst the clouds.

It is this freedom that allows us to be of service. We break the illusion of giving and receiving for our service comes from copious amounts of love. We learn of service from those who heal their connection with nature. It is when nature is drawn to us that we become of service to the Great Mother. We do not lose sight of our power by medicating our gifts. It is when we are stung by death and survive that we realise that emptiness is more beautiful than existence. The spell of slavery is lifted from our purity.

It is purity that allows us to access our gifts, the blessings that have been bestowed upon us the moment we took our first breath.

The young girl who lives in ancient Nordic lands has a reverent attraction to the forest. It is a cloudy afternoon when she discovers that she can commune with the spirits of the forest. The plants speak to her of their magical healing qualities. The girl begins to collect certain herbs, twigs and mushrooms from the pharmacy of the woods, one that is hidden in plain sight. One day her boyfriend does not meet her where they had planned. Her patience fades and she decides to walk back home. On her way back she is informed that her boyfriend's father is terribly ill. She immediately sets on foot to her boyfriend's residence. On her way, her attention falls on a milkweed that speaks to her of its healing properties. She does not have time for this nonsense. There are more important matters at hand. She arrives at the house that is silent. The father speaks his final words. His son is to scatter his ashes on the land to the far north where he was born. The old man silently perishes from heart failure. Life goes on. The young girl is now a woman studying folkloric herbs. In her course, she learns of the medicinal uses of milkweed for heart conditions. She remembers the day, years before, when the milkweed had spoken to her. Had she listened, perhaps a life would have been saved? Regardless, it was on that particular day that the plant had spoken to her. Then and there, she accepts her gift of communing with the forest. There are things that she encounters in her life that she may never understand. She will not attempt to invent explanations when there are none; she will simply trust and observe what follows. She begins to talk openly to her folkloric teachers of the plants that she collected in her childhood. Her teachers confirm the medicinal properties of the plants she had assembled intuitively, because we know our gifts when we are young.

The young lad from Ireland is easily irritated by common conversations. He finds himself always walking away when people get into any form of discussion. He thinks people talk too much. People think he is quiet because he has nothing important to say. Yet the young lad does not speak because the conversations move too fast for him to assemble the words that seem to come from so many different layers of intellect. The information in his head is far too noisy for him to express himself with any integrity. One day the weight of information he carries in his head implodes and he is suddenly left with the emptiness that comes when intellect is erased. It is then that he is able to speak of that which is immediately profound. He accesses the intelligence of ancient traditions from the memories of eternity, the intelligence that induces silence because we begin to mediate upon the words that are spoken.

As long as our gifts are hidden from us, the system will make perfect sense. Those who discover their gifts find it very difficult to live amongst those who haven't. It is when we fully accept our path of service that we are granted our gifts. We can never learn the gifts; they are only available in the moment. This is perhaps how magic is protected from destructive ends. The apparently meaningless rituals of honouring the earth, each other and ourselves are there to purify our intentions. Rituals remind us that we are of this world and so are our gifts. It is through ceremony that we honour our gifts. Ceremony reminds us that we are all here for each other. It is by coming together in song and dance that we offer ourselves to love. Ceremony keeps the flame burring in our hearts. Without ritual and ceremony, the sun may rise but if we do not wake up early, we may miss the beauty that reminds us that today is not just another day. And so we make the most of our gifts by healing each other and in doing so, we acquire qualities that we may never have discovered otherwise. Healing and expansion are the same thing, one cannot exist without the other. If we do not share our gifts, we continue to seek validation from doing things. We begin to live a sort of half-life because we have been persuaded out of respecting our hearts. By honouring our gifts we let go of trying to be anyone other than ourselves. Until then, we may not realise how much benefit we can be to another.

The older brother brings joy to hearts wherever he goes. He has the uncanny ability to make someone smile even when they don't want to. The younger brother is never far behind. He wants to be like the older brother but lacks the qualities that make his older brother so mighty. The younger brother is far too conscious of what other people feel to be as confident as his brother. One day they are visiting their uncle who has a playground in his backyard and adventurous cousins to play with. The older brother is received warmly by his cousins while the younger brother is seen only as his shadow. The younger brother decides to stay inside while the other boys chase their adrenaline-filled adventure. The uncle sees the younger brother sitting alone in the corner.

'Are the boys not giving you love?' he asks the boy. The little brother says that he never feels good enough to play with the older brother. The uncle explains that we all have our own qualities. The more we try to be someone else, the less satisfaction we find in ourselves.

'What good is it being myself when no one likes me?' asks the boy.

'We are all loved for different reasons. Your older brother may spark delight wherever he goes but he never cleans up the mess he leaves behind. You, boy, are too considerate to create a mess. Your love for others will create incredible friendships. They will be far richer than those based on the worshipping of so-called friends we think of as better than us.'

It is by accepting our own gifts that we truly come into our power. Our gifts are there to open the doors in the hearts of many. The tree does not keep its fruits for itself. It is by being of service that we come to enjoy the fruits of our existence. It is when we share our gifts that love and service become one.

Angel of Inca - Story of rising within

'He became a part of my life quite unexpectedly. But the moment I met him I knew we were going to do great things together,' says Alice to her family. The train they were on entered a tunnel as they headed deeper into the highlands of Peru. Alice was in these very mountains only three months ago. She had been travelling for adventure and was attracted by the lost cities of the Inca. Back then she did not expect things to change so quickly.

When she went off a trail during her last trip, she discovered the doorways hidden in the mountains. One of the doorways was carved into a rocky mound the size of a school bus. Perhaps it was curiosity that led her to peek inside. She quickly stepped back the moment she saw what was inside. Worried someone might have spotted her, she stood silently, perhaps out of some remnant form of respect. She will just walk away and tell no one. As she walks, her eyes steal an unwilling glance into the doorway. It is too late now. They are all looking at her. Alice is surprised that instead of awkwardness, she feels an overwhelming warmth coming from the people inside the cave. She doesn't know what comes over her as she marches straight into the doorway and enters a tomb-like cave. No one says anything to her. They resume their casual chatter as if nothing important had happened. Alice walks across the cave and sits by herself with her back against the cave wall. She notices the people around her. There are roughly 20 people and they seem to be from all over the world. Then she sees him, a gentle soul looking at her and whispering into the ears of the man next to him. He sees that she is now looking at him and gives a gentle nod to greet her, then resumes his conversation. Alice does not know what to make of this gathering. However, she feels no urgency to leave this sacred tomb.

The night sky begins to descend upon the earth. A trace of anxiousness begins to unsettle Alice. It is then that the gentle soul gets up. All conversations slowly end and they all follow him out of the tomb. The men light up a few torches with fire and Alice follows them down a trail that she had not noticed until then. They arrive at a little village made up of a handful of rudimentary huts. They enter one of the larger huts and prepare some food. Alice is given a bowl of corn soup and some bread. Alice suddenly realises how hungry she had been. After supper, one of the women leads Alice to an empty hut. She lights the candle inside and gives her a warm blanket. 'Rest sweet, my dear,' she tells Alice and then quietly walks out of the hut. Alice gets into bed. Her mind momentarily drifts to her travel plans. She's to be back in Lima in the next two days to catch her flight to Bolivia. The trip to Bolivia does not make sense anymore and with that Alice falls into a deep sleep.

It feels like years have passed when Alice wakes up the next morning. She quickly races out of her hut, hoping that she has not been left behind. Her eyes take a moment to adjust to a scene that she had not yet seen in daylight. It's as if the village had been expecting her. The woman who had shown her the hut embraces Alice and asks for her to ground some quinoa. Throughout the day Alice finds herself doing primitive activities with utmost fascination. She learns that the gentle soul's name is Andres. She learns that Andres was chasing his dream of becoming a clinician in Buenos Aires when, he accidentally discovered the miraculous healing effects he had over people. One of his patients had come into his clinic, engulfed in fury. He had been deceived into committing a crime and was now faced with costly fines. His patient demanded anti anxiety medication. Alice learned that Andres simply placed his hand on the patient's shoulder and an overwhelming sense of peace descended into him. His patient was then able to think clearly and they worked together on the steps that cleared the criminal charges against him. Alice is intrigued by the story but does not take it too seriously.

It is mid afternoon when Andres approaches Alice. His presence has an immediate soothing effect on Alice. Andres does not say anything, they simply walk together in the direction of the mountains, bathing in each other's presence. Then an abrupt movement next to her catches Alice's eyes. She looks down to see an injured rhea, a flightless bird found in these regions. The bird is in a state of shock and seems to have escaped the notorious grip of an eagle. Andres crouches down and the bird instinctively walks into his hands. Andres picks the bird up and the rhea falls asleep in Andres' hands as they continue their walk.

'You fear your gift, because you have blocked out the times when you thought you saw ghosts in your childhood. Since then, you've thought magic does not exist and the world can be explained,' says Andres.

Alice stops walking. She looks at Andres with a mild distaste. 'What do you know about me?' says Alice and then with a bit more annoyance she says, 'I've seen many things in my life. I've travelled many places. All you know is the mountains. We live in a world that has advanced with technology that creates jobs and treats the ill. I'm valued in my industry and I know that sitting around, waiting for magic to happen gets you nowhere.' Alice herself is surprised by the force with which she had spoken the words. She sees that the rhea in Andres hands is awake now.

Andres crouches back down. He releases the rhea and as if by magic, the wings of the rhea seem to be working perfectly well. Alice quickly dismisses what she has just witnessed. She starts walking back to the village, leaving Andres behind.

'Let me help you,' she hears Andres say. But she ignores him and keeps walking. She spends the night in the village and then continues with her travels in South America. She travels through Bolivia, Chile and Argentina before returning home to San Francisco.

Alice is happy to be back home and is hired again in her previous job. Her contract is for a month, as a film producer. She works late each night finishing a short film on the voyage of three men who sail their self-made yacht from the Greek Islands to the Bahamas. One evening, a co-worker, John stays on to help Alice with some cut scenes. While they are working together, Alice feels an unbearable irritation from John. 'What is wrong with you?' the words come out of Alice's mouth before she realises what she is saying. Slightly taken aback, John tells her that he has had chronic neck and shoulder pain ever since he remembers. He tells her that he has seen countless doctors and therapists. He has even had surgery at two different hospitals to no avail. Alice feels concerned about John and offers him a little massage at the end of the night.

Alice and John continue working for another two hours and then they walk back to Alice's apartment. Alice places a mat on the floor and asks John to lie comfortably on it. She lights a few candles and a sandalwood stick. John closes his eyes and the exhaustion of the day weighs on his body. The calming atmosphere transports Alice back to the hills in Peru. The soothing effect that she felt there now begins to transpire through her. Her intention to massage John somehow feels inappropriate now; something is stopping her from doing so. Visions begin to appear into Alice's mind. Without thinking Alice begins to speak out these visions. Her voice puts John into a hypnotic trance.

Alice asks John to imagine walking in a magnificent savannah at night. She asks him to imagine the stars descending into the grassland until the earth below his feet disappears. Only the universe remains. The universe that exists within him. She asks John to travel to the centre of this universe. At the very centre, she asks him to find a doorway. 'Open the door and walk inside,' she says. 'The doorway leads to a staircase winding down. Walk all the way down. At the very bottom you will find a library with many books. Each one is a past life. This is where I leave you,' says Alice. 'You may choose a book and it will show you what you need to know,' says Alice.

Only a minute passes before Alice feels the inclination to end the experience. She guides John out of the dreamlike state. It takes another few minutes before John sits back up. There is an awkward silence between them. In order to break the tension, Alice asks if John is ok. John merely nods his head, then gets up and walks out of the apartment. Alice feels a little embarrassed by what she has just performed. The whole process seemed to come out of nowhere.

The next day, she is surprised when she sees John at work. Not only is John feeling great but it looks as if he is leading the team with boundless passion. John spots Alice and comes running over.

'I have to tell you what happened,' he says to Alice. They both walk aside and then John begins to share his story.

'At first I thought this was all strange. I found it difficult to imagine but there was something about your voice that put me at ease. I found myself floating in space even before you started talking about the universe. By the time I got to the library, I knew exactly which book to pick up. When I opened the book, I found myself in a medieval city square with hundreds of people looking at me. I was in the centre of the square, seconds away from being executed. I only had a few seconds to act. In that moment, I appeared as my current self and looked deeply into the eyes of my former self and said, "I forgive you". Just then I was hung. That is when I heard your voice guiding me out of my experience. After I left your apartment I caught a taxi and went straight home. This morning I woke up feeling like an enormous weight had been lifted off my shoulders. Better still, all my neck pain has disappeared. I don't care how or why. I simply feel great. I can't remember the last time I felt this way.'

John gives Alice a massive hug. He then springs back into action with the team. John's story leaves Alice with a sense of depth within herself that she had often dismissed in order to relate to daily life. She works for two more weeks till the end of the documentary project. With no more work lined up, she decides to experiment with these so-called gifts. She finds that she can voluntarily enter the trance-like state whenever it is needed. She finds herself miraculously healing those around her through gifts she did not know she had: the gifts of touch, spontaneous words of wisdom and irrefutable revelations.

People from many walks of life begin to come to Alice. Not all are convinced or satisfied with what they receive, yet each experience allows Alice to gain deeper insight into her gifts. Alice works like this for another two months until one day, she feels a sharp pain in her stomach. She ignores the pain and continues her day as scheduled. When she is working on her last session for the day, she starts feeling nauseous. Moments later she collapses to the ground. Her client immediately calls an ambulance.

When Alice wakes up, she finds herself at the UCSF medical centre.

Alice does not know what is going on. She wants to ask for help, but words seem to escape her tongue. It is then that she sees her mother crying with a doctor outside the patient's room. The doctor sees that Alice is awake, walks into the room and sits beside her. Her mother stays at the door but looks away.

'You have pancreatic cancer. You will be lucky if you live past the next two weeks,' says the doctor. At first Alice does not believe the doctor's words. She tries to read more from the doctor's expression yet everything tells her that his words are true. She is too stunned to cry. The doctor leaves the room and her mother walks in. She sits beside her daughter. Her mother's face is broken from the tears that speak the words her lips are unable to say. Alice reaches out to her mother and they embrace, making up for years of scarce contact when they were both too busy with their lives.

'Mum. I want to go to Peru. I think there is someone who can help me,' says Alice. Her mother is wary of the little time she has with her daughter but does nothing to object her last wish. Alice's father cancels his work commitments in San Diego and the family gets on the plane to Peru. They arrive in Lima and from there catch the train to visit the gentle soul in the mountain. They pass through a tunnel and stop in a small town for the night. Alice's mother wakes up with a grave feeling the next morning. She looks at Alice lying in her bed. She softly calls to her husband to wake up. Alice's father looks into the eyes of his wife and tears begin to drip from his eyes. Their daughter had taken her last breath while they were sleeping. News of Alice reaches the village with the gentle soul. Andres arrives at the town where Alice's family was. Her parents momentarily feel a sense of ease from his presence. Andres asks them if he can attend their daughter's funeral.

Back in San Francisco, there is a tremendous outpour of support for Alice's family. The flood of letters and condolences begin to arrive from friends and family near and far. More than 500 people attend her memorial. Her close friends and family share stories of love and humour

Then Andres shares his poem[28]:

You walk your chosen path
with elegance
the part of your soul
that is visible to others
Your work is the
manifestation of love
each moment with
dedication and care
for others.
Your unspoken prayer
The offering you call service.
In your last heartbeat
You didn't squander
this life
a blessing
Touching the heart of many
through the words you sing
You chose service
With eyes that forever
sparkle with happiness
Shining forth with
the light of love
Contagious and unapologetic
The hearts of many will

28 In memory of Jo Mall from *A Sound Life*

finish what you began
The seeds you scattered
Will enlighten the generation
Yet to come
You devoted to service
with courage and humility
A road without
a goal to be reached
But one of
selfless love
Until one day
the road stopped
He who can arrive at
any hour, without warning
You greeted him with love
when he knocked on your door.
O' Lead me
To the truth
From darkness
To the light
This body
to eternal life
O' lead me
to you.
In the final second,
when life gives you your last breath,

It does so with terrible guilt
For you understood that small things
are responsible for great changes.
And for that reason,
Without a choice in the matter
He asks you to come with him
To light a new star
Unable to go back
and recover lost moments
Tomorrow the sun
will rise again.
Om Shanti.

It is not the words of Andres that touch the people, but the fathomless love that comes from his heart, which confuses them. In this event of great grief, Alice's friends and family are unable to reconcile what they are feeling. Can love and grief exist all at once? How can you miss someone when all you feel when you think of them is love? They realise they are not grieving Alice's death but celebrating her life, a life of service that offered nothing less than love. The energy that Alice lived her life with was present even in her death. The love and generosity we share continue to flow, long after we have perished.

⋆ ⋆ ⋆

End and means are one. So we already know how it all ends. Do we still wait to be of service in the future when we have the 'means' to do so? Life is a journey. We walk as far as our legs can carry us and when we look back we will see that service is in every moment. It is when we serve that we fulfill our prophecy.

Journey of Remembering

Who I am
and where
I want to be
are the same thing
The beginning
is inseparable from
the end

~ Self Quote

When we return to our true nature, we experience that which predates time. How then is life a journey when we are both its source and simultaneously moving towards it?

We may convince ourselves of nonsense such as moving forward, evolving and achieving. When we see the impossible done effortlessly, we call it success. However, the evolutionary experiment of nature is trivial and does not lead to success. The evolution of thought has not led us to become self-aware. The purity of consciousness was already all-knowing, through and through. It is time to remember, Holy one. To become the star that was once stone. The heavens, they sing and the Angels, they dance to the pure vibration of love. They sing for freedom, they sing for peace, they sing for us to shine in all our grace. They sing to rejoice the love that fills this space.

The day Man decided to build their own kingdom, they forgot the architecture of the great intelligence. Man forgot that all is provided for and started to create out of lack. Man decided that they knew better, so they created need. By separating ourselves from the Great Mother, we have forgotten where we belong. We have replaced the great intelligence with machine and invested our lives to work tirelessly in vain. So we turn around and look back at our magical realm. We return home, to be cuddled in the arms of our Great Mother. To be locked in embrace with God. We walk on this earth, this kingdom of love. We open our hearts to who we have always been. Oh great majesty, the divine creation of love, please remember all that is time is an illusion. Start to remember, Holy one, we are the voice of love, the voice of God, our each and every footstep blessed and so loved.

When we fall on our knees and pray for all our troubles to go away, we are praying to leave our illusions behind. We pray because it did not matter how much we 'tried to work it out', it amounts little to the choice we must make now: to let go of the hand of illusion. The affair with the mind gave us pleasure while it lasted, but truth has a habit of flowing out of our hearts. The mind may give up as it often does, but the purity of the heart is here to stay. So let's walk amongst the Angels on the noble path of the heart.

We remember that the purity of our hearts protects us from illusion. Our extraordinary magnificence aligned with the intention of creation. Our intelligence is decentralised and integrated with the pure vibration of love. Our unbearable reverence for each other uplifts our capacity to commune with the consciousness that is all-knowing. We no longer speak of that which we know. What we know is of little interest to us. We instead draw on the secrets of the universe from one another, the key to unlocking the mysteries of the magical realms. We feel each other's hearts beating, the wonderful feeling of softness that is soothing. Nature responds to our beating heart. The mysteries of the heart, no different to that of the universe. Nature becomes visible only when we wake up from our dream and come to realise that the greatest paradox is that we are able to comprehend paradoxes. The sun burns with our light, the interconnected exchange of energy that circulates between you and me. The light emitted from the heart of men, inseparable from the stars that shine. Light: the highest frequency of love. Truth: the highest frequency of thought.

Holy one, our ascension is our highest intention, the only hope to end this human 'race'. Let's stop the confusion of playing chess with the light and dark. We cannot defeat ourselves. We are the lover, we are the loved and we are the love within everyone. We are the dance of the divine filled with the purest of vibrations. We open our hearts to break any resistance to who we have always been. Holy one, we love you so. As the sun shines through the clouds, this is the time to dance by each other's side. We find ourselves in our hearts, all the time. The place we all belong. We are not Buddha, we are not Elijah, let us not play small. Inseparable from the source, we are God, the holy transmission of love.

Speak to me of Sacred Ceremony

We do not do ceremony out of lack. If we seek an experience, we interfere with the realm of the sacred. We already are all there is, it is then ceremony seeks us. For those who have become the noble mind of God, heaven opens for them. It is our purity to which the ceremony reveals itself. We realise that ceremony is not for ourselves; we are already abundant and free. Ceremony seeks us because we are the physical manifestation of the greatest power in the universe. It is through ceremony that we reconfigure any energy that has been misaligned or tries to control spirits that are lost. Ceremony does not heal us. It is we who are ceremony, existing now as creation.

This noble service of ceremony has now been robbed of its sacredness. Shamans and other gatekeepers of magical portals abuse substances, which they call medicine in exchange for money. This is no different to our modern medical industry that creates disease for profit. False shamans offer experiences to those who seek in lack. The participants then return back to their homes, only to struggle with the experience of the sacred and that of daily life. The struggle exists as long as both these forces exist in the same body. May we remember to take the only medicine there is: the medicine of the heart. There is no force in the universe that love cannot heal. Only when we surrender to the noble path of the heart, are we welcomed by the Angels. We are blessed with the sacred opportunity of human ascension. Heavens doors are unlocked on the path of noble intention.

Speak to me of the Age of technology

How can we harm the Great Mother and call it progress? Do we not see the cost of our creation? With our dependence on primitive technology we drive for innovation. We speak of doing less bad rather than more good. Our separation from the noble path creates problems that we expect technology to solve. We merge our senses with primitive machines such as handheld and wearable devices that decapitate us from the Great Intelligence. The technology of ancient civilisations[29] have been far more advanced than what we have today. Our technology has paralysed us and disabled the evolution of our intelligence to one that is machine-like: linear, automated and repetitive.

We may speak of artificial intelligence, virtual and augmented realities. However, these takes us deeper into an artificial reality. We move further from the magic we experience from visceral connections and lose ourselves in a bionic mental landscape. We forget that our technologies are human-centric. The human brain has not sworn allegiance to the human body. In virtual reality, the human brain is able to coordinate movements of forms that are not anthropomorphic, a lobster for example. Organisms that have been able to decentralise their nervous system have been granted immortality. The jellyfish (*Turritopsis dohrnii*) for example, is able to revert to earlier stages of their life cycle and remain immune to age and disease. The subconscious intelligence of the human body can, to a certain degree, be decentralised for autonomy of multiple body parts. In the Russian combat technique known as Systema, a single person can face multiple combatants simultaneously without ever having to think centrally. To decentralise and exist simultaneously in every cell of our body may be our antidote to death. Our body may be in perfect shape, however, if a vital organ fails, the nervous system may decide to forfeit life. The evolution of a centralised brain occurred when earth creatures first became bilateral. Somehow, two faces looking in different directions got glued together to the same body. We gained the two hemispheres of the brain. Then, men asked the questions, 'Who am I?' The mind of God cannot ask this question of them-self.

29 Referring to Egyptian and Mayan technologies.

Technology is the product of our lack. The lack that exists because of our human centric existence. Nature is responsive to the intelligence of the whole. To date, there isn't a single technology that can reproduce the energy-harvesting capacity of a single cell, let alone a whole organism. We have created nothing that has not already existed before us. Nature has been 3D printing the moment the universe decided to split in two to contemplate itself. The masculine and feminine come together to create that which no technology in existence can reproduce. We close off our senses and look through the eyes of primitive technology for intelligent life. We search the universe through the pigeonhole of a telescope in an effort to abandon the kingdom of God.

In the 15 year quest to find proof for his equations on the General Theory Relativity, Albert Einstein said: "I want to know God's thoughts, the rest are details." In a similar period in history, Srinivasa Iyengar Ramanujan [30]- one of the greatest mathematician's to have lived said "An equation for me has no meaning, unless it expresses a thought of God". Perhaps it is communion with the invisible that brings forth the greatest insights of humankind. The formless possibilities of the human consciousness are far reaching yet have been reduced to machine-like computation by primitive man-made machines. Regardless of which planet we are on, we will destroy it as long as the purity of our consciousness is diluted by lack. Oh Holy one, how have we forgotten that it is the Great Intelligence that we search for in the heavens above. The Angels and countless manifestations of pure consciousness communicate with us. Open your hearts and hear them sing.

Today, remotely operating nanotechnology can be used to reverse transcribe information into our neuronal DNA[31]. The entities that work to control us are widespread and have been subconsciously manipulating us through all of our senses. The purity of consciousness can neither be

30 See - The Man who Knew Infinity (film).

31 See - BRAIN Initiative (Brain Research through Advancing Innovative Neurotechnologies)

controlled nor destroyed. This moment is inseparable from who we are, who we've always been from the very beginning. We embody the mind of God in this formless body. Holy one, open your hearts and become the sun. May our fire bring warmth to the heavens above. May we fill the endless expanse of the universe with the light of our heart. The technological storm will pass. May we be free from the mass extinction of all that is illusion.

Speak to Me of the Quest for Knowledge

In our ascension, concepts, knowledge and dogma fail to gives us meaning. We have little interest in what we know. We have even less interest in contemplating what comes from the lack. We instead become clear channels for angels to speak through us. Some may embody the consciousness of planetary systems, others may embody the consciousness of animal spirits, others still may embody the consciousness of ascended ones. We embody and are simultaneously in reverence of the holy ones. Oh Jesus, oh Mary Magdalene, oh Radha, oh Krishna, oh Vishnu, oh Lakshmi, we honour the intelligence that has been transmitted to us. By being a clear channel we can become any consciousness we choose. We see then that the only consciousness that can fill our vastness is that of God. Fallacies of the mind dissolved in the presence of unavoidable truth.

We open ourselves to who we truly are, who we have always been, from the very beginning. There are no questions that we don't already know the answer to. It is in this moment, that we become so precise. The first conception of thought reveals all; each and every thought unto itself. Our brains are evolving from the cognitively heavy simulation of future possibilities based on past experiences (explicit thinking) to one that holds all possibilities live in real time. All is revealed, all at once (implicit intelligence). Our minds may vaguely translate what we channel into words, but it is not the words that matter, it's the state in which they are spoken. The vibration of truth, the purest vibration within me and you. In this moment we become the mind of God, the endless expanse existing simultaneously in all locations and periods of time. The breath of God, translated for us by the Angels who love us so. It is when thought begins to precipitate, that the vibration of love begins to fill this space. It is this energy of love through which we build our sacred Kingdom.

SPEAK TO ME OF OUR KINGDOM

Our hearts are inseparable from nature, just as lovers are from each other. As the rain falls on our heads in the open wind, we demand each other's attention. We dance with the sacredness of divine creation. Oh Great Mother, we dream of you: the great intelligence that exists for all of us to see, the intelligence of a perfect loving system. Captured by the beauty of pristine creation, we are freed from the illusion of separation. We are stripped naked in the presence of God. The great temple of God - our very home. Nature is God's kingdom in its pristine state.

In the immaculate kingdom of God, breath connects us with the skies above. The heavens expand our consciousness beyond the realms held by this ancient earth. As we open our hearts and breathe, we fulfill the ancient prophecy; to surrender to our divinity. The great intelligence giving conviction to our every step. We see the fruits: they grow by themselves as nature's great offering to honour our existence. We fall in love with the sweet waters as we surrender to the dance of the sun and the moon. The birds sing the great love song; the butterflies dance to the sacred harmony of all there is. To all there will ever be. The kingdom of God is here for you and me, for all to see. It's in our hearts that we find prosperity.

All in good time, the magical realms, we will find. The portal opens for the fairies to come through. Dear one, open you hearts and you shall see that human ascension is the key to our prosperity. The purity of the unknown is found in realms that are thought-free. The certainty of mind will not allow the unknown to unfold. The drive for success and achievement will exist in the dimension of linear thought. As long as illusion defeats the purity of consciousness, we may never reconnect with the parts of ourselves that our senses have been closed off to. To the brothers and sisters, the flowers and the creatures that the Great Mother speaks through, oh how we have forgotten you. In the Holy vibration of love, our senses are returned to us. It is light that the pure beings are attracted to. We welcome Angels to feel their support. The kingdom is here. The kingdom that ancestor upon ancestor dreamt of. To this kingdom we sing the songs of honouring. The ancient remembrance: this kingdom of God.

Speak to Me of Our Destiny

The Great Sage climbs up the Mountain. He has lived so long that he stopped measuring his age. When he was young, his Mother jokingly called him a sadhu - which in Sanskrit means holy man. His Father once said to him that the world will take everything away from you except your knowledge. As a child he was quick to recognise that we suffer because we build our hopes and dreams from that which creates an apocalyptic future. The future we create on the planet that we destroy each day. The starving man does not think of fixing the world's problems. He has his own mouth to feed. Yet it is not he who starves, it is the land that has been striped of its natural abundance.

The Great Sage sees that like all children of the Great Mother, he must one day grow up. He sees that the rite of passage for every human being is to wake up from the human condition. He sees that many have woken up. The human experience for them is no longer an evolutionary experiment in survival. They free themselves from the human condition that breeds disease and suffering. They see the world through the eyes of forgiveness and their vulnerability allows them to speak truth. They are throwing away the shields that protects their hearts. The Great Sage sees that when Love justifies the rest of their days, there is no way they can fail. The Great Sage learns to do the same. His mind surrendered, refusing to flee from love. His body Alive, to continue the journey.

The Great Sage learns that nothing ever happens for a reason because we invent reasons for the lessons we think the universe is teaching us. We may think we are part of some grand plan, yet the plan is simply a wishful dream. The Garden of Eden was doing fine until the universe decided to create Man and Woman. Unable to find a use for their mind, they abandon the Tree of Life and ate the Forbidden Fruit from the tree of Knowledge. Poisoned by knowledge, Man and Woman begin to thirst for More. Lack appears where love once was. Under the spell of knowledge, they begin the quest for meaning. The Great Sage sees that Magic has a way of finding us when we abandon the search for meaning. It is then that the Great Sage experiences life with excruciating pleasure. Each moment overwhelms him with gratitude. Magic is no longer a possibility but a daily reality. On his way to the top of the Mountain, a child stops the Great Sage and says, 'You look like you are contemplating your soul. What if we ate from the Tree of Life?' The Great Sage smiles for a moment and then replies, 'We already have. The tree of life has cast the spell of time and took away our immortality.' The Great Sage then asks Time, 'Magic does not play by your rules. Are you not offended?' To this Time says, 'I am of your own making. You may think that cycles exists because of me. But I guarantee no certainty. For as long as I exist, we repeat the cycles of birth and death. Powerful societies may rise. Prophets may appear. We may believe our consciousness to alter into higher states. It is in these altered states that we bend time and space. And because Magic cannot be understood, some get terrified and demonise Magic. It is then that we hunt, torch and outlaw those who act in ways that do not fit our explanations. As with all cycles, it starts all over again.'

The child on the Mountain interrupts the thoughts of the Sage and asks,

'What is our purpose?' The Great Sage assesses the question then says, 'When you say "what is" it suggests the existence of something. When you say "our" it suggests that it exists because of us. When you say "purpose" it suggests that there is a reason for the existence of this "something". If we assume that the "something" is "us" then "what is" and "our" are referring to the same thing. And because "purpose" is inseparable from who we are - every word refers to the same thing. This my child, is how language has fooled us into thinking.' The child ignores the Great Sage. He has no patience for perplexities.

The Great Sage continues on his climb up the Mountain. There are many paths to the top, some more difficult than others. For the Great Sage however, there is no step more important than the one he is taking right now. He reaches the top of the Earth. His body so light that he floats on air when he decides to sit. Suspended between the visible and the invisible the Great Sage greets Death as it approaches him without hesitation. Death consumes his physical form in this life, the afterlife and all other attempts he has made to exist in Time. The Great Sage is no longer "great" nor a "sage". In this moment he is closer to his soul than he has ever been before.

In a state of surrendered love, he begins to see through the eyes of his soul. He sees that the ups and downs in life were simply the shower of kisses that universe provides. There were times in his life that he fiercely pushed forward, yet it was only when he decided to quit, that he discovered something deeper. Since then, he would feel a burst of energy whenever he did anything that would bring him closer to his soul. Yet, he sees that to his soul it did not matter if he lived a life that was practical, adventurous or full of bitterness. Unbound by form, the soul has the remarkable ability to split its consciousness an infinite number of times. The first time the soul split in two, Man and Woman appeared in the Garden of Eden. In order to better understand each other, the two souls decide to eat from the Tree of Knowledge. However, the more they ate, the more they discovered how little they knew.

Unable to comprehend the meaning of life, they decide to eat from the Tree of Life. Offended by their reckless consumption, Death appears and curses them with Time. In order to defeat Time, the two souls decide to self-propagate, yet no amount of life is immune to Death. So the Souls decide that life must be lived in a manner that is unpredictable, so Death will find it difficult to intercept their journey. Without a meaning to live for, the souls asks Pain to accompany them on their journey. And since suffering continues its cycle with each generation, we begin by forgiving. The soul then redeems itself in each life in one of four ways - in the depths of grief and suffering. The soul finds itself when we surrender to the ecstasies of sex. The soul finds itself when we surrender to perpetual meditation. The soul finds itself through portals at the cusp of death. Through the great act of surrender, the soul sees that pain causes no suffering. We then become transformative agents for Magic. We use our Gifts to heal the world. Yet, even Magic is governed by certain laws:

To revoke the curse of knowledge, Magic asks us to forget everything that we know. To prevent us from explicitly performing magic based on past experiences, Magic cannot be learnt. It arrives precisely as required by the moment. To be free of desire and temptation that leads to reckless consumption, Magic can only be performed from altered states. The decision to use magic is not ours therefore, Magic cannot be used for the benefit of ourselves or others. Magic is in service of the divine order. We cannot use Magic when we are in Pain. It is purity that grants us access to Magic. Light, the purest vibration of Love. Truth, the purest vibration of thought. We do not explain Magic because the Tree of Life does not offer its secrets easily and the meaning of Life remains a mystery. In the noble path of the heart, we do not shield ourselves from the pain of others, because we are protected by purity and cannot be controlled by energies that have been misaligned.

We are the chosen ones because we exist and we have discovered who we truly are. Gone is the age of rockstars and gurus. The day has arrived when we completely accept our gift of Magic. We feel as if we have crossed a threshold. The point of no return. With our soul fully shining through us, we see that we are not alone. We see others that have done the same. They have abandoned the dreams that shrivels their soul. The dreams they had once inherited from systems designed to suffocate the soul. May our spirits be lifted by the prospects of the battle ahead. We blame no one for the steps we didn't take, because we thought no one could. We take that step Now for our soul to remain intact. The sovereignty of our soul reveals our destiny. Those trapped in pain will doubt their power, only because they think they stand alone. Those who have crossed the threshold of no return, stand together at the frontier of the universe. The cities, they need us the most and there is no where else to go. We do not sit back and watch our Great Mother suffer. We protect the Garden of Eden, the great valley of souls. The Tree of Life and the Tree of Knowledge are right in front of us to show that time and money are currencies of lack. We exchange one illusion for another. The illusion of lack seduces us with the temptation that our dreams may one day come true. When we return to the arms of our Great Mother, we find that Magic has always been around us - this moment that is hidden in plain sight. The sovereignty of our every breath is our destiny. The magic of love erupts from our soul that is inside. This Ancient Remembrance - The Inside Story of the Soul.

Magical Realms - Story of our Kingdom

'Don't be afraid. As long as you follow you heart, the angels will always light your way,' he replies. Evan takes his eyes of his soulmate. He looks to the mountain ahead of him. He does not need to take the canoe this time. He shall walk back home to the grand architecture of Mother Nature. Evan miraculously found this cave when he went travelling after quitting his job at the environmental NGO.

That one night with Sarah on his birthday, three years ago, had reminded him of a part of himself he did not want to acknowledge. Sarah had said, 'It is this light at the bottom of the well that is the eternal flame of love.' He remembers how the madness of love had pushed him to the edge of a cliff. The love that breaks our hearts, until we give up what we love the most. Be it who we love. It is then that we completely lose ourselves to love.

Sometimes, people don't merely cross our path, they change our whole direction. Evan thinks of Zara. Perhaps the magical experience of last night was because her journey is new; because she sees the world with the eyes of a child. There have been times in his life when Evan thought he had met his soulmate. This is what he thinks - oh, how easily does the mind fool the heart into dismissing magic! Magic is always present in moments that we fail to explain.

Evan stops for a moment. His mind is still on Zara even though she is on her way to Vietnam. He feels the ancient land he stands on. His body relaxes. This moment becomes ceremony. He looks to the sky and once more calls upon Zara's soul. He asks for all the energies that may have been exchanged, experiences that may have joined and anything that may stand between them to be liberated and returned back to them in the purified state of love. The psychological channels between them are closed off and protected forever from any wounds or scars through which their energy may be drained. Evan feels himself magnifying in strength, freed from all prisons of duality. He feels his consciousness dematerialise back into the formless. He once again becomes the elevated essence of God.

The lightness in his step returns as he springs effortlessly up the mountain; his cheerful smile greeted with the gentleness of the nature around him. He arrives at his cave, the grand cathedral, as ancient as the land of God. The morning light filters through the natural curtains of the forest. The granite walls of the cave, as high as the sky, twinkle with the countless crystals embedded within it. Evan feels a profound silence that dissolves him into nothingness. He lowers himself to the ground just before he is knocked out and loses consciousness...

'Where am I?' The blurry scene becomes visible in the thick carpet of fog. In front of him lies a pile of rubble and a giant man who had bled to death due to a blow to his head. The name Razul comes to mind. Perhaps it is related to this giant man? He decides to walk away from this desolate village but then notices that there is one house still standing. He walks towards it. As he remembers the name Razul as his own, he instantly feels the warmth of home. He opens the rugged wooden door and walks inside. The house is of modest built and appears to be from the 17th century. He sees a man and woman in the kitchen looking at him. He feels some aggression from the man but recognises the woman instantly. It is Zara. She recognises her previous husband but pretends not to know him. Instead of withdrawing into emotion, Razul feels an unending strength: the eternal strength of love. Zara's resistance begins to fade. Her unbearable love for Razul returns and she throws herself into his arms. The other man is powerless to stop her and slowly his presence fades from existence. Razul and Zara are left alone in the kitchen. Razul, the noble warrior united once again with the one he holds dear. With a noble heart, he has faced the dark. The channel opens up for communion with the invisible and the messages begin to flow:

'The warrior loves because he has been alone. He has been broken. He has cried without end. The warrior knows that pain and suffering are sign posts pointing towards love. The warrior loves because he has found no other way. The courage to fall in love is his greatest strength. The warrior's courage burns fiercely in his heart. The energy that can no longer be contained in his lover's presence. The true reason for passion becomes alive. Two become one. Time comes to an end. What we experience surpasses definitions and rules. Shameless in our wildness, what we experience predates our own DNA. It is through love that nature intended new life to be born. It is through love that we ascend beyond this world.

'The warrior is devoted to a path of service. Money, power and greed are temptations too small for a warrior's heart. Ever since he accepted the path of his heart, his path has been running towards him, greeting him in his every step. The warrior has little interest in proving his strength; yet his strength never fails him because its source is surrender. With each opportunity to surrender, he loses a part of himself but not spirit; spirit is found in the human body and the warrior finds comfort in embodiment. He dedicates his own expertise to the all-knowing intelligence that works through him. The warrior does not wait for the universe to provide. He is the universe. He is the creator. He has no interest in living tomorrow as if it were yesterday. Illusions of past and future cannot withstand his devotion to this moment. The warrior sets his intention, the noble path that he commits to in this moment. The warrior is not distracted by that which does not honour light. Entities are neither good nor bad, but simply catalysts on the path back to light. The great intelligence unquestionable to the once doubtful heart. The warrior's heart is the master key to all of Heaven's doors.'

The Holy remembrance awakens in the two lovers' hearts, in this life, past lives, in all locations and periods of time. Razul, a warrior whose touch knows no violence. Zara the embodiment of the feminine, so held, adored, loved and protected. The great joy they experience is the height of our existence.

The dream fades and Evan becomes aware of his body once again. The earth feels assuring below him. He does not feel like moving. He simply lies there, integrating the information contained in his dream. It does not matter if the events were real or not. His subconscious is profoundly reprogrammed by the information he received. Perhaps, it is in our dreams that the wisdom of ancestors is revealed.

Zara feels an eruption of love in her heart on her boat trip back to the mainland. It's as if her heart has been opened from afar. She cannot explain it, but it seems like it is raining love and everything she sees is radiating love back at her. She does not even know his name yet she feels as if a cycle has come to an end and like all cycles, it will begin again.

Upon arriving in Vietnam, the explosion of love overwhelms her. As she leaves the airport, she sees a billboard with a white-water rafting adventure. Zara does not waste much time at her hostel, she arranges with a local driver to take her to the rafting adventure the next morning. Young and free, she is up for anything. The next morning, she sets off on a three-hour journey inland through rugged country. She learns that the white water flows through a narrow canyon that was split in half after an earthquake millions of years ago. It is still early morning when they arrive at the canyon and the tourist centre is not at all busy. She is asked to wait until more people arrive for the adventure.

Zara does not wait long. Within moments, two girls arrive, sleepy yet excited for an adventure. Their guide walks them down the steep forest path until they arrive at a clearing around a softly flowing river. The guide and Zara sit on one side of the raft while the two girls sit on the other. While they float down the river, the guide asks them to put on their lifejackets before the rapids. He explains the paddling sequence. The scenery changes exquisitely as they flow out of the forest and enter the canyon. The walls of the canyon are lined with waterfalls and fluorescent moss and lichens. Zara cannot believe her eyes; tears begin to flow as she witnesses the magic of nature. Their raft gains momentum. They are approaching the rapids. All of a sudden, the guide shouts at the girls to grab the paddle and steer the raft with the little control that they have. The raft bounces and bumps along the rocks as it spins out of control in the white water. The feeling is terrifying and exhilarating at the same time; Zara sees terror in the eyes of the guide. He has little time to react when the raft hits an obscured log and everyone is catapulted into the air. Miraculously, they all land in waist-deep water without injury. The guide quickly collects the girls and they form a chain as the rapids carry them. The guide spots a narrow bank and thrusts the girls onto land. He then climbs out of the water, frightened and confused.

With their raft lost, they have little hope of returning to safety without help. The guide suggests that they wait for help to arrive. The girls agree with him for no more than 30 seconds as their little group begins getting swarmed by mosquitoes. Very quickly they all get agitated and begin to climb up the canyon wall along self-planned routes. The wall is moist and slippery but there is little time to reflect. Quickly, the two girls reach the top while the guide stays back, waiting for Zara to climb out of the canyon first. As she is making her way up, Zara suddenly stops, perplexed, and sees that the twig she was holding onto a second before is no longer attached to the canyon wall. She is floating mid-air! Why isn't she falling? She tries to regain her balance, quickly readjusting her footing, when she notices a luminous purplish-blue fairy the size of her lifejacket, sitting on lichen. Her mind instantly interjects and desperately tries to define what she is seeing. In rapid succession, she thinks 'dragonfly', 'butterfly', 'bird', but refuses to believe what her eyes are picking up. With a shy smile, the fairy springs off the lichen and flies out of sight. When it disappears, so does the image of what it looked like. Zara's mind suppresses what she cannot believe. She looks down to her guide and asks him whether he saw anything fly. He did, he replies and says it vaguely resembled a purple butterfly but was somehow too big to be one. Zara quickly climbs up to the top of the canyon.

They all walk back to the tourist centre and report the accident. Zara interrupts the report and starts to describe the incident with the fairy but very quickly cuts herself short when she sees the looks on everyone's face; they think she is mad.

Back at her hostel, Zara desperately searches the internet for fairies but cannot find anything close to what she has seen. In fact she can hardly remember what the fairy looked like. To believe in magic would contradict everything her mind agrees with; still Zara cannot get it out of her mind. She spends the following day on her computer researching articles on fairies. By evening, as she is starting to lose interest, she comes across an article by a Dr. Evan Hunter and begins to read his research on wildlife protection. She discovers that he has left his industry, in frustration. He writes that deforestation and globalization affects not only the habitat of common wildlife, but also that of other unseen beings of light; those creatures are departing the forest and finding elsewhere to go. Zara reads about little blue angels that displace time to divert the path of he who can arrive at any moment.

'Who is this crazy Evan Hunter?' she thinks to herself. She clicks on the 'about' page and to her disbelief, the photo shows the mysterious mountain man she had met only a few days ago. She remembers his last words.

Angels have guided her heart to experience what her mind refuses to believe in. Yet, Zara is intoxicated with what she cannot explain. Weeks, months, years pass by as she digs up ancient information. Information that is attractive to the mind but rarely satisfies the heart. With her heart as her only guide, she begins to integrate her own information, because when we talk of what no one believes in, we clear our own path to truth. Her relentless passion gives her life direction. She starts a movement advocating the protection of unharmed land.

Zara acquires certain qualities that allow the forces of nature to work with her. Her senses begin to pick up on subtleties in the energy of different forests. She learns that by not paying attention to wildlife, its inhabitants become comfortable with her presence. More peculiar creatures begin to reveal themselves and soon the fairies appear again. They appear in places where sacred energy is strong. Those are not popular places with heavy tourist traffic but magical spots found in unharmed forests. Each fairy has a certain magical quality. They appear on their own accord and assist anyone whose will is not against the continual expansion of consciousness. The magic of fairies never creates anything new; instead the reality perceived is reconfigured in each moment. Zara's consciousness begins to reach places where her mind thought there was none.

Magic propels Zara into the heart of organisations wishing to shift the trajectory of cooperations from global suicide to global resurrection. Zara is able to provide detailed information of underground water channels that supply cave systems in Mexico. She talks about the forest intelligence communicated through the root systems of ancient trees. She identifies the acoustic shields assembled by marine beings in the great ocean to protect cetaceans and other intelligent life from the deafening sounds of military sonic bombs that map the position of every submersible in the ocean. Zara's work catches the interest of the European Eco Summit. She gets invited to their upcoming annual conference in Geneva. Zara spends many nights organising the information she will present. When she arrives at the conference, she feels a monumental sensation similar to what she felt when she arrived in Vietnam. Then she sees him. The opening plenary talk of the conference is by Dr. Evan Hunter. Zara is overwhelmed by his presence. All the information she had collected to this point perishes. Everything that she knew fell short of what she sees in Evan. In fact, Zara does not register a word Evan says. Like her first experience with the purplish-blue fairy, her mind tries to describe who she is seeing: mountain man, wildlife expert and lover? Her consciousness begins to expand to meet his. As her mind is stretched beyond its capacity, she feels an unending void taking its place. Love erupts from her heart to fill the void in her consciousness. All at once, she understands everything.

When it comes to Zara's time to talk, she abandons all that she knows and speaks directly from the mind of God. It does not matter what she says, words are simply thoughts in the form of vibration. The frequency coded in each word she speaks shifts the state of each person in the room, including the spirits of the ancestors who walk beside her. As above, so below. Here we are now in the kingdom of God.

After the conference, Zara changes all her plans to return with Evan to the cave where it all began. To Zara's amusement, when they reach the top of the cliff where they spent their magical night, she discovers that this was only the outer overhang to the entrance of the cave. They walk along the narrow edge of the cliff - which opens up into a 3-walled living area overlooking the vast ocean, the soil floor of the cave, soft like a sheepskin carpet. The sunlight reflecting of the crystalline cathedral feels as if the rock is glowing from within. At the end of the living room is a naturally created archway leading to the next section of the cave. At the centre of this room is a stone stove and a simple wooden shelf along one of the walls. The kitchen opens up to the edge of the cliff where she finds a two layered wooden platform which somewhat resembles a tree house. The first layer stores some books, clothes and musical instruments. The second layer is lined with amber and red cushions and a soft mattress under the open sky. The platform brings warmth to the hardness of the crystalline rock. The vastness of the cave means that it is always well-lit yet sheltered from the strongest winds and rain.

Evan removes all his clothes as if it is the most natural thing to do. Zara does the same and at once feels more connected to the earth than she ever had. Without her clothes, she feels the freedom of a newborn, rid of any social definitions, stories about herself and the need to hide. The paradox of being so free yet so connected bewilders Zara.

'My Queen,' she hears Evan say. 'In the magical realm we are free of human psyche. When we are in the presence of the purest of nature, loneliness disappears. This is the paradox. The density of human psyche is the source of loneliness in overpopulated cities. Let's not deny that we feel our each and every footstep is protected by the Great Mother. The holy vibration of love, the essence of our kingdom. My Queen, it is in our kingdom that we find sovereignty in every breath. You will always be free,' says Evan.

In the days that follow, Zara experiences profound shifts in her daily patterns. The purity of the edible plants that Evan gathers from the forests makes her food cravings disappear. Her morning begins at 2am, when important messages are received. She falls asleep soon after they have been written and wakes up to the sunrise. She finds that her mind is silenced by the immensity of the rocks around her.

One afternoon when Evan returns from gathering firewood from the forest, Zara says to him, 'I don't feel like speaking much anymore. Am I losing the ability to have a conversation?'

Evan sits down with her and takes her hand. 'What do we speak of when there is nothing to be said? It is the unnecessary dependence on conversations that fills up our lack. Conversations disappear when the purity of our consciousness exceeds the threshold of the mind. Then we tap into the ever-present consciousness of angels. Some call this creativity. I call this the intelligence of the higher order.'

Zara feels unsatisfied with his answer. 'So we sit around in a cave doing nothing and commune with angels?' she asks.

'What are the messages you have been receiving?' asks Evan.

'To go back to the city and share my message. I don't have anywhere to pour my passion when I live in a cave,' she replies.

'Then return you must. It is not we who return to the forest, but it is when the forest returns to the cities that we have truly regained our kingdom,' Evan replies.

'I'm afraid. I don't think I can be as free in the city as I am here,' says Zara.

'The magical realm does not exist as physical space. The magical realm is the kingdom of your heart. The fairy became visible in Vietnam because in your heart, you felt that it was raining love. When love justifies the rest of our days, there is no way we can fail,' replies Evan.

'My soul spoke to me last night and I don't want to leave my soulmate again,' cries Zara.

'We can never leave, because you can never be mine. I'm not in love with you. My love is deeper than that. I'm committed to love itself. It is the absence of love that is the real distance between two people. Biologically, conditions could not be more favourable for us. You may be my cave-wife and I, your caveman. However, it is how we dance past each other that is more magical than sitting together forever. Besides the cave is not our only home, I have a beautiful friend April, who has a treetop villa in the Serengeti National Park in Tanzania. We work together to heal our relationship with our Great Mother,' replies Evan.

Zara moves closer and rests her head on Evan's shoulder.

'My Queen, love does not fade when the sun goes down at night. Love turns into romance when the sun is replaced by fairy-flies. In our sacred union we are immaculate in our conception of the purest of seeds. Time has no meaning when the forest cannot tell whether it is day or night. Perhaps this is why love prefers twilight,' is all he says.

★ ★ ★

Oh divine majesty, fill up the universe with pure love. It is this moment that we have all been waiting for. To become the sun, chosen one. Radiate your life-giving light to heal the Great Mother. To rid her of the toxins that drain her spirit. My earth, we heal for you. We look to the sky so that the golden eagle may once again fly. We look to the sea so that the great whale may remember the songs of their ancestors. We look to the mountains to fill them with love so that they may reach to kiss the sky. We look to the forests for magic, the noble force working with our own nature. We take sovereignty of every breath. When we come into our power, we realise that we have just begun. Open your hearts and breathe, this is the universal prophecy. Our quest for meaning only began when we decided to invest in illusion. Now that our illusion has proved to be such an unlucrative business, perhaps it's time to erupt with laughter. The laughter that shakes the universe as it spreads where there was nothing. The laughter that creates the plants and planets, the galaxies and other impossible things. We laugh for illusion will refuse to make sense.

EPILOGUE

Readers may wonder on the accuracy of the information and events described in this book. I've written this book in a manner that is cognitively nonlinear, presenting the information in multiple layers so to speak not to the intellect but to the subconscious. I claim no validation for what I say. Instead I leave it up to the reader to decide what they believe to be true. The truth will resonate in your own heart; and that is also the case for what will not.

Note on the information

Science will continue to fragment reality into measurable units. Each time we subtract from reality we get further from truth. The micro-units of reality in science laboratories are validated through statistical theorems. These theorems give a probability of truth of a subjective reality under controlled conditions. The sensitised and clinically conditioned thought patterns of scientists work within a single plane of reality, which is known as rationality. Science is too small a paradigm for me to explain that which lies beyond rationality. Many have tried to explain the supernatural using quantum physics, neuroscience and the like and in doing so have destroyed the magic of the unexplained. By viscerally embodying intelligence, I wish to convey multilayered information that we can connect to emotionally, viscerally and subconsciously.

As long as the mind finds things to believe in, we will continue to seek validation. The deeper our beliefs, the more validation we seek. Because we have fragmented ourselves by creating an identity around our beliefs, it is the loose piece of illusion that we use to build the walls behind which we elude ourselves. Only when we are stripped of illusion do we embody the purity that is perception-less. I do not wish for you to believe what I say. That would be a terrible tragedy. Instead, I have written this book so that magic can be experienced viscerally. Once we begin to embody this information, the mind no longer seeks validation for the unexplained. I offer no final conclusion because I know nothing. Only then am I able to write without motive and speak of that which is closest to our hearts.

Note on the stories

All stories in this book are works of fiction derived from historical events from the author's own experience. Although the events through which each story is assembled are fictional, the experiences are real.

I have had many experiences working with clients which I may never have an explanation for. Neither do I wish to explain such occurrences, because in doing so I immediately interfere with the possibility of magic. Each time I am working with a client, it is a new journey for both of us. I can provide no information on what I will do, because I rely simply on the guidance of the moment. I can offer no benefits because it is only after the sessions that the client informs me of benefits that I could not have imagined. We have no control over the outcome, no matter how much we plan. There is nothing to cure but simply miracles of the moment as we discover the world together. This is why I let go of the outcome and trust in the process. I trust blindly without doubt or fear. It is this trust that allows my clients to shed the psychological and visceral blocks that may interfere with the process. Then at the client's own will, I push them in the direction of their freedom until there is nothing left to impede who they truly are.

Simply because we are unable to scientifically validate what we cannot measure does not refute the existence of phenomena beyond our cognitive threshold. The purpose of these stories is to demystify the supernatural and lift the taboo on the nonsensical aspect of our reality. Paradigms shifts are often met with resistance because they are simply mental constructs of illusion. I choose to remain in a state of wonder rather than offer a new paradigm. I do not need to understand magic to work with miracles. Besides, change is inevitable so breaking our own rules is also important.

★ ★ ★

May we drink from the waters of love that flow from the tears that have healed us. May we live in the enchanted forests where humankind can evolve undomesticated. May we climb mountains simply to break our own perspectives so that we can meditate upon the unknown. May our magic be unbroken like the lullaby that takes us to lands where dreams are made. May we be drunk with the ecstasy of love to undo the global suicide and go beyond the cycles of birth and death. May we dance in the strength of our beauty in gratitude of life. Just because we exist, we have made it.

Dr. Kaushik Ram world leading neuroscientist, his seminal work on the nervous system teaches us about the subconscious and how to naturally elicit intuition, gut instincts and creative insights. His masterful mix of science and poetry allows us to self-assemble the pieces of the subconscious puzzle in an undeniably efficient manner.

Social Handles (Facebook, Twitter, Instagram)

@DrKaushikRam

Be Published

Publish through a successful publisher.
Brolga Publishing is represented through:

- **National** book trade distribution, including sales, marketing & distribution through Dennis Jones & Associates.
- **International** book trade distribution to
  - The United Kingdom
  - North America
  - Sales representation in South East Asia
- Worldwide e-Book distribution

Order

HIDDEN WORLD
The Inside Story of the Soul

ISBN: 9781925367867	Qty	.....
RRP	AU$24.99	.....
Postage within Australia	AU$5.00	.....
TOTAL*	$....	

* All prices include GST

Name: ....

Address: ....

Phone: ....

Email: ....

Payment: ❑ Money Order ❑ Cheque ❑ MasterCard ❑ Visa

Cardholder's Name: ....

Credit Card Number: ....

Signature: ....

Expiry date: ....

Allow 7 days for delivery.

Payment to:

Marzocco Consultancy (ABN 14 067 257 390)
PO Box 12544
A'Beckett Street, Melbourne, 8006 Victoria, Australia
markzocchi@brolgapublishing.com.au